MICHAEL HERR was born in Syracuse, New York, and attended Syracuse University. In 1967, he went to Vietnam as a war correspondent for *Esquire* magazine. There, without any restrictions, he roamed the war-ravaged countryside watching, looking, listening, and writing it all down.

DISPATCHES

Michael Herr

AVON
PUBLISHERS OF BARD, CAMELOT, DISCUS AND FLARE BOOKS

Grateful acknowledgment is made to the following for permission to reprint previously published song lyrics:

ABKCO Music, Inc.: Specified eleven words from the song "2000 Light Years From Home" by Mick Jagger and Keith Richard. (p. 250) Copyright © 1967 by ABKCO Music, Inc. Also, specified seven words from the song "Citadel" by Mick Jagger and Keith Richard. (p. 250) Copyright © 1967 by ABKCO Music, Inc. All Rights Reserved. International Copyright Secured. Reprinted by permission.

American Broadcasting Music, Inc.: Specified two lines of lyrics from the song "San Francisco (Be Sure And Wear Some Flowers In Your Hair)" by John Phillips. (p. 131) Copyright © 1967 by American Broadcasting Music, Inc., and Honest John Music. Used by permission only. All Rights Reserved.

Arc Music Corp.: Specified ten words from the song "Good Morning, Little Schoolgirl" by Sonny Boy Williamson. (p. 259) Copyright © 1964 by Arc Music Corp. All Rights Reserved. Used by permission.

Comet Music Corporation: Specified twenty words from the song "Magical Mystery Tour" by John Lennon and Paul McCartney. (p. 114) Copyright © 1967 by Northern Songs Limited. All rights for the U.S.A., Canada, Mexico, and the Philippines controlled by Comet Music Corporation. All Rights Reserved. Used by permission.

Cotillion Music, Inc.: Specified seven words from the song "The Tighten Up" by Archie Bell & The Drells. (p. 9) Copyright © 1968 by Cotillion Music, Inc., and Orellia Publishing Co. Also, specified seven lines from the song "For What It's Worth" by Stephen Stills. (p. 147) Copyright © 1966 by Cotillion Music Inc., Springalo Toones and Ten-East Music. All Rights Reserved. Used by permission.

Dwarf Music Specified two lines of lyrics from the song "Visions of Johanna" by Bob Dylan. (p. 223) Copyright © 1966 by Dwarf Music. All Rights Reserved. Used by permission.

Frank Zappa Music, Inc.: Specified six lines of lyrics from the song "Trouble Comin' Every Day" by Frank Zappa and the Mothers of Invention. (p. 233) Copyright © 1965 by Frank Zappa Music, Inc. All Rights Reserved. Used by permission.

Contents

Breathing In

There was a map of Vietnam on the wall of my apartment in Saigon and some nights, coming back late to the city, I'd lie out on my bed and look at it, too tired to do anything more than just get my boots off. That map was a marvel, especially now that it wasn't real anymore. For one thing, it was very old. It had been left there years before by another tenant, probably a Frenchman, since the map had been made in Paris. The paper had buckled in its frame after years in the wet Saigon heat, laying a kind of veil over the countries it depicted. Vietnam was divided into its older territories of Tonkin, Annam and Cochin China, and to the west past Laos and Cambodge sat Siam, a kingdom. That's old, I'd tell visitors, that's a really old map.

If dead ground could come back and haunt you the way dead people do, they'd have been able to mark my map CURRENT *and burn the ones they'd been using since '64, but count on it, nothing like that was going to happen. It was late '67 now, even the most detailed maps didn't reveal much anymore; reading them was like trying to read the faces of the Vietnamese, and that was like trying to read the wind. We knew that the uses of most information were flexible, different pieces of ground told different stories to different people. We also knew that for years now there had been no country here but the war.*

The Mission was always telling us about VC

contact or anything that even sounded like contact would give me more speed than I could bear. Whenever I heard something outside of our clenched little circle I'd practically flip, hoping to God that I wasn't the only one who'd noticed it. A couple of rounds fired off in the dark a kilometer away and the Elephant would be there kneeling on my chest, sending me down into my boots for a breath. Once I thought I saw a light moving in the jungle and I caught myself just under a whisper saying, "I'm not ready for this, I'm not ready for this." That's when I decided to drop it and do something else with my nights. And I wasn't going out like the night ambushers did, or the Lurps, long-range recon patrollers who did it night after night for weeks and months, creeping up on VC base camps or around moving columns of North Vietnamese. I was living too close to my bones as it was, all I had to do was accept it. Anyway, I'd save the pills for later, for Saigon and the awful depressions I always had there.

I knew one 4th Division Lurp who took his pills by the fistful, downs from the left pocket of his tiger suit and ups from the right, one to cut the trail for him and the other to send him down it. He told me that they cooled things out just right for him, that he could see that old jungle at night like he was looking at it through a starlight scope. "They sure give you the range," he said.

This was his third tour. In 1965 he'd been the only survivor in a platoon of the Cav wiped out going into the Ia Drang Valley. In '66 he'd come back with the Special Forces and one morning after an ambush he'd hidden under the bodies of his team while the VC walked all around them with knives, making sure. They stripped the bodies of their gear, the berets too, and finally went away,

back. He died before he could tell us what happened."

I waited for the rest, but it seemed not to be that kind of story; when I asked him what had happened he just looked like he felt sorry for me, fucked if he'd waste time telling stories to anyone dumb as I was.

His face was all painted up for night walking now like a bad hallucination, not like the painted faces I'd seen in San Francisco only a few weeks before, the other extreme of the same theater. In the coming hours he'd stand as faceless and quiet in the jungle as a fallen tree, and God help his opposite numbers unless they had at least half a squad along, he was a good killer, one of our best. The rest of his team were gathered outside the tent, set a little apart from the other division units, with its own Lurp-designated latrine and its own exclusive freeze-dry rations, three-star war food, the same chop they sold at Abercrombie & Fitch. The regular division troops would almost shy off the path when they passed the area on their way to and from the mess tent. No matter how toughened up they became in the war, they still looked innocent compared to the Lurps. When the team had grouped they walked in a file down the hill to the lz across the strip to the perimeter and into the treeline.

I never spoke to him again, but I saw him. When they came back in the next morning he had a prisoner with him, blindfolded and with his elbows bound sharply behind him. The Lurp area would definitely be off limits during the interrogation, and anyway, I was already down at the strip waiting for a helicopter to come and take me out of there.

"Best way's to just keep moving," one of them told us. "Just keep moving, stay in motion, you know what I'm saying?"

We knew. He was a moving-target-survivor subscriber, a true child of the war, because except for the rare times when you were pinned or stranded the system was geared to keep you mobile, if that was what you thought you wanted. As a technique for staying alive it seemed to make as much sense as anything, given naturally that you were there to begin with and wanted to see it close; it started out sound and straight but it formed a cone as it progressed, because the more you moved the more you saw, the more you saw the more besides death and mutilation you risked, and the more you risked of that the more you would have to let go of one day as a "survivor." Some of us moved around the war like crazy people until we couldn't see which way the run was even taking us anymore, only the war all over its surface with occasional, unexpected penetration. As long as we could have choppers like taxis it took real exhaustion or depression near shock or a dozen pipes of opium to keep us even apparently quiet, we'd still be running around inside our skins like something was after us, ha ha, La Vida Loca.

In the months after I got back the hundreds of helicopters I'd flown in began to draw together until they'd formed a collective meta-chopper, and in my mind it was the sexiest thing going; saver-destroyed, provider-waster, right hand–left hand, nimble, fluent, canny and human; hot steel, grease, jungle-saturated canvas webbing, sweat cooling and warming up again, cassette rock and roll in one ear and door-gun fire in the other, fuel, heat, vitality and death, death itself, hardly an intruder. Men on the crews would say that once you'd car-

still smoking, and something between your chest and your stomach would turn over. Frail gray smoke where they'd burned off the rice fields around a free-strike zone, brilliant white smoke from phosphorus ("Willy Peter/Make you a buh liever"), deep black smoke from 'palm, they said that if you stood at the base of a column of napalm smoke it would suck the air right out of your lungs. Once we fanned over a little ville that had just been airstruck and the words of a song by Wingy Manone that I'd heard when I was a few years old snapped into my head, "Stop the War, These Cats Is Killing Themselves." Then we dropped, hovered, settled down into purple lz smoke, dozens of children broke from their hootches to run in toward the focus of our landing, the pilot laughing and saying, "Vietnam, man. Bomb 'em and feed 'em, bomb 'em and feed 'em."

Flying over jungle was almost pure pleasure, doing it on foot was nearly all pain. I never belonged in there. Maybe it really was what its people had always called it, Beyond; at the very least it was serious, I gave up things to it I probably never got back. ("Aw, jungle's okay. If you know her you can live in her real good, if you don't she'll take you down in an hour. Under.") Once in some thick jungle corner with some grunts standing around, a correspondent said, "Gee, you must really see some beautiful sunsets in here," and they almost pissed themselves laughing. But you could fly up and into hot tropic sunsets that would change the way you thought about light forever. You could also fly out of places that were so grim they turned to black and white in your head five minutes after you'd gone.

That could be the coldest one in the world, stand-

could shoot bullets, moving and antsing and shifting around inside their fatigues. "No sense us getting too relaxed, Charlie don't relax, just when you get good and comfortable is when he comes over and takes a giant shit on you." That was the level until morning, I smoked a pack an hour all night long, and nothing happened. Ten minutes after daybreak I was down at the lz asking about choppers.

A few days later Sean Flynn and I went up to a big firebase in the Americal TAOR that took it all the way over to another extreme, National Guard weekend. The colonel in command was so drunk that day that he could barely get his words out, and when he did, it was to say things like, "We aim to make good and goddammit sure that if *those guys* try *anything cute* they won't catch us with our pants down." The main mission there was to fire H&I, but one man told us that their record was the worst in the whole Corps, probably the whole country, they'd harassed and interdicted a lot of sleeping civilians and Korean Marines, even a couple of Americal patrols, but hardly any Viet Cong. (The colonel kept calling it "artillerary." The first time he said it Flynn and I looked away from each other, the second time we blew beer through our noses, but the colonel fell in laughing right away and more than covered us.) No sandbags, exposed shells, dirty pieces, guys going around giving us that look, "We're cool, how come you're not?" At the strip Sean was talking to the operator about it and the man got angry. "Oh *yeah?* Well fuck *you,* how tight do you think you want it? There ain't been any veecees around here in three months."

"So far so good," Sean said. "Hear anything on that chopper yet?"

often as it fattened and darkened in accumulating alienation. It was great if you could adapt, you had to try, but it wasn't the same as making a discipline, going into your own reserves and developing a real war metabolism, slow yourself down when your heart tried to punch its way through your chest, get swift when everything went to stop and all you could feel of your whole life was the entropy whipping through it. Unlovable terms.

The ground was always in play, always being swept. Under the ground was his, above it was ours. We had the air, we could get up in it but not disappear in *to* it, we could run but we couldn't hide, and he could do each so well that sometimes it looked like he was doing them both at once, while our finder just went limp. All the same, one place or another it was always going on, rock around the clock, we had the days and he had the nights. You could be in the most protected space in Vietnam and still know that your safety was provisional, that early death, blindness, loss of legs, arms or balls, major and lasting disfigurement—the whole rotten deal—could come in on the freaky-fluky as easily as in the so-called expected ways, you heard so many of those stories it was a wonder anyone was left alive to die in firefights and mortar-rocket attacks. After a few weeks, when the nickel had jarred loose and dropped and I saw that everyone around me was carrying a gun, I also saw that any one of them could go off at any time, putting you where it wouldn't matter whether it had been an accident or not. The roads were mined, the trails booby-trapped, satchel charges and grenades blew up jeeps and movie theaters, the VC got work inside all the camps as shoeshine boys and laundresses and honey-dippers, they'd starch your fatigues and burn your shit and then

ning on their hands and knees toward the grass where it wasn't blown flat by the rotor blades, not much to be running for but better than nothing. The helicopter pulled up before we'd all gotten out, leaving the last few men to jump twenty feet down between the guns across the paddy and the gun on the chopper door. When we'd all reached the cover of the wall and the captain had made a check, we were amazed to see that no one had even been hurt, except for one man who'd sprained both his ankles jumping. Afterwards, I remembered that I'd been down in the muck worrying about leeches. I guess you could say that I was refusing to accept the situation.

"Boy, you sure get offered some shitty choices," a Marine once said to me, and I couldn't help but feel that what he really meant was that you didn't get offered any at all. Specifically, he was just talking about a couple of C-ration cans, "dinner," but considering his young life you couldn't blame him for thinking that if he knew one thing for sure, it was that there was no one anywhere who cared less about what *he* wanted. There wasn't anybody he wanted to thank for his food, but he was grateful that he was still alive to eat it, that the motherfucker hadn't scarfed him up first. He hadn't been anything but tired and scared for six months and he'd lost a lot, mostly people, and seen far too much, but he was breathing in and breathing out, some kind of choice all by itself.

He had one of those faces, I saw that face at least a thousand times at a hundred bases and camps, all the youth sucked out of the eyes, the color drawn from the skin, cold white lips, you knew he wouldn't wait for any of it to come back. Life had made him old, he'd live it out old. All those faces, sometimes it was like looking into

DMZ that was firing support for Khe Sanh, and the truck had hit a Command-detonated mine, then they'd been rocketed. The Marines were always running out of things, even food, ammo and medicine, it wasn't so strange that they'd run out of bags too. The men had been wrapped around in ponchos, some of them carelessly fastened with plastic straps, and loaded on board. There was a small space cleared for me between one of them and the door gunner, who looked pale and so tremendously furious that I thought he was angry with me and I couldn't look at him for a while. When we went up the wind blew through the ship and made the ponchos shake and tremble until the one next to me blew back in a fast brutal flap, uncovering the face. They hadn't even closed his eyes for him.

The gunner started hollering as loud as he could, "Fix it! Fix it!," maybe he thought the eyes were looking at him, but there wasn't anything I could do. My hand went there a couple of times and I couldn't, and then I did. I pulled the poncho tight, lifted his head carefully and tucked the poncho under it, and then I couldn't believe that I'd done it. All during the ride the gunner kept trying to smile, and when we landed at Dong Ha he thanked me and ran off to get a detail. The pilots jumped down and walked away without looking back once, like they'd never seen that chopper before in their lives. I flew the rest of the way to Danang in a general's plane.

II

You know how it is, you want to look and you don't want to look. I can remember the strange feelings I had when I was a kid looking at war

M-16 on full automatic starting to go through clips, a second to fire, three to plug in a fresh clip, and I saw a man out there, doing it. Every round was like a tiny concentration of high-velocity wind, making the bodies wince and shiver. When he finished he walked by us on the way back to his hootch, and I knew I hadn't seen anything until I saw his face. It was flushed and mottled and twisted like he had his face skin on inside out, a patch of green that was too dark, a streak of red running into bruise purple, a lot of sick gray white in between, he looked like he'd had a heart attack out there. His eyes were rolled up half into his head, his mouth was sprung open and his tongue was out, but he was smiling. Really a dude who'd shot his wad. The captain wasn't too pleased about my having seen that.

There wasn't a day when someone didn't ask me what I was doing there. Sometimes an especially smart grunt or another correspondent would even ask me what I was *really* doing there, as though I could say anything honest about it except "Blah blah blah cover the war" or "Blah blah blah write a book." Maybe we accepted each other's stories about why we were there at face value: the grunts who "had" to be there, the spooks and civilians whose corporate faith had led them there, the correspondents whose curiosity or ambition drew them over. But somewhere all the mythic tracks intersected, from the lowest John Wayne wetdream to the most aggravated soldier-poet fantasy, and where they did I believe that everyone knew everything about everyone else, every one of us there a true volunteer. Not that you didn't hear some overripe bullshit about it: Hearts and Minds, Peoples of the Republic, tumbling dominoes, maintaining

place where they go around with war in their heads all the time.

"If you get hit," a medic told me, "we can chopper you back to base-camp hospital in like twenty minutes."

"If you get hit real bad," a corpsman said, "they'll get your case to Japan in twelve hours."

"If you get killed," a spec 4 from Graves promised, "we'll have you home in a week."

TIME IS ON MY SDE, already written there across the first helmet I ever wore there. And underneath it, in smaller lettering that read more like a whispered prayer than an assertion, *No lie, GI*. The rear-hatch gunner on a Chinook threw it to me that first morning at the Kontum airstrip, a few hours after the Dak To fighting had ended, screaming at me through the rotor wind, "You *keep* that, we got *plenty*, good *luck!*" and then flying off. I was so glad to have the equipment that I didn't stop to think where it had to have come from. The sweatband inside was seasoned up black and greasy, it was more alive now than the man who'd worn it, when I got rid of it ten minutes later I didn't just leave it on the ground, I snuck away from it furtive and ashamed, afraid that someone would see it and call after me, "Hey numbnuts, you forgot something. . . ."

That morning when I tried to go out they sent me down the line from a colonel to a major to a captain to a sergeant, who took one look, called me Freshmeat, and told me to go find some other outfit to get myself killed with. I didn't know what was going on, I was so nervous I started to laugh. I told him that nothing was going to happen to me and he gave my shoulder a tender, menacing pat and said, "This ain't the fucking movies over

me, no one had ever looked at me like that before. I felt a cold fat drop of sweat start down the middle of my back like a spider, it seemed to take an hour to finish its run. The man lit a cigarette and then sort of slobbered it out, I couldn't imagine what I was seeing. He tried again with a fresh cigarette. I gave him the light for that one, there was a flicker of focus, acknowledgment, but after a few puffs it went out too, and he let it drop to the ground. "I couldn't spit for a week up there," he said, "and now I can't fucking stop."

When the 173rd held services for their dead from Dak To the boots of the dead men were arranged in formation on the ground. It was an old paratrooper tradition, but knowing that didn't reduce it or make it any less spooky, a company's worth of jump boots standing empty in the dust taking benediction, while the real substance of the ceremony was being bagged and tagged and shipped back home through what they called the KIA Travel Bureau. A lot of the people there that day accepted the boots as solemn symbols and went into deep prayer. Others stood around watching with grudging respect, others photographed it and some just thought it was a lot of bitter bullshit. All they saw out there was one more set of spare parts, and they wouldn't have looked around for holy ghosts if some of those boots filled up again and walked.

Dak To itself had only been the command point for a combat without focus that tore a thirty-mile arc over the hills running northeast to southwest of the small base and airfield there from early November through Thanksgiving 1967, fighting that grew in size and fame while it grew more vicious and out of control. In October the small Dak To Special Forces compound had taken some

ent started to write that down and the paratrooper said, "Make that 'little pieces.' We were still shaking the trees for dog tags when we pulled back out of there."

Even after the North had gone away, logistics and transport remained a problem. A big battle had to be dismantled piece by piece and man by man. It was raining hard every day now, the small strip at Dak To became overloaded and unworkable, and a lot of troops were shuttled down to the larger strip at Kontum. Some even ended up as far out of their way as Pleiku, fifty miles to the south, for sorting and transport back to their units around II Corps. The living, the wounded and the dead flew together in crowded Chinooks, and it was nothing for guys to walk on top of the half-covered corpses packed in the aisles to get to a seat, or to make jokes among themselves about how funny they all looked, the dumb dead fuckers.

There were men sitting in loose groups all around the strip at Kontoum, hundreds of them arranged by unit waiting to be picked up again and flown out. Except for a small sand-bagged ops shack and a medical tent, there was no shelter anywhere from the rain. Some of the men had rigged up mostly useless tents with their ponchos, a lot lay out sleeping in the rain with helmets or packs for pillows, most just sat or stood around waiting. Their faces were hidden deep inside the cover of their poncho hoods, white eye movement and silence, walking among them made you feel like you were being watched from hundreds of isolated caves. Every twenty minutes or so a helicopter would land, men would come out or be carried out, others would get on and the chopper would rear up on the strip and fly away, some toward Pleiku and the hospital, others back to the Dak To area and

I goes like, 'Never happen, Sir.*' So he does, he goes up there himself and damned if the fucker didn't get zapped. He said we was gonna have a real serious talk when he come back, too. Sorry 'bout that."*

"Kid here [not really here, "here" just a figure of speech] gets blown away ten feet in back of us. I swear to God, I thought I was looking at ten different guys when I turned around. . . ."

"You guys are so full of shit it's coming out of your fucking ears!*" one man was saying.* PRAY FOR WAR *was written on the side of his helmet, and he was talking mostly to a man whose helmet name was* SWINGING DICK. *"You were pissing up everything but your fucking toenails, Scudo, don't you tell me you weren't scared man, don't you fucking* dare, *'cause I was right fucking* there *man, and I was scared* shit! *I was scared every fucking minute, and I'm no different from any body else!"*

"Well big deal, candy ass," Swinging Dick said. "You were scared."

"Damn straight! Damn straight! You're damn fucking straight I was scared! You're about the dumbest mother-fucker I ever met, Scudo, but you're not that dumb. The Marines *aren't even that dumb man, I don't care, all that bullshit they've got in the Marine Corps about how Marines aren't ever afraid, oh wow, I'll fucking bet. . . . I'll bet the Marines are* just as scared!*"*

He started to get up but his knees gave under him. He made a quick grasping spasm out of control, like a misfire in the nervous system, and when he fell back he brought a stack of M-16's with him. They made a sharp clatter and everyone jerked and twitched out of the way, looking at each other as though they couldn't remember for a minute whether they needed to find cover or not.

waiting and that he'd come out to see if he could draw a little fire. What a look we gave each other. I backed out of there fast, I didn't want to bother him while he was working.

This is already a long time ago, I can remember the feelings but I can't still have them. A common prayer for the over-attached: You'll let it go sooner or later, why not do it now? Memory print, voices and faces, stories like filament through a piece of time, so attached to the experience that nothing move and nothing went away.

"First letter I got from my old man was all about how proud he was that I'm here and how we have this *duty* to, you know, *I* don't fucking know, whatever . . . and it really made me feel great. Shit, my father hardly said good morning to me before. Well, I been here eight months now, and when I get home I'm gonna have all I can do to keep from killing that cocksucker. . . ."

Everywhere you went people said, "Well, I hope you get a story," and everywhere you went you did.

"Oh, it ain't so bad. My last tour was better though, not so much mickeymouse, Command gettin' in your way so you can't even do your job. Shit, last three patrols I was on we had fucking *orders* not to return fire going through the villages, that's what a fucked-up war it's gettin' to be anymore. My *last* tour we'd go through and that was it, we'd rip out the hedges and burn the hootches and blow all the wells and kill every chicken, pig and cow in the whole fucking ville. I mean, if we can't shoot these people, what the fuck are we doing here?"

Some journalists talked about no-story operations, but I never went on one. Even when an operation never got off the ground, there was al-

fresh, and a couple of times you'd even hear something high, like the corpsman at Khe Sanh who said, "If it ain't the fucking incoming it's the fucking outgoing. Only difference is who gets the fucking grease, and that ain't no fucking difference at all."

The mix was so amazing; incipient saints and realized homicidals, unconscious lyric poets and mean dumb mother-fuckers with their brains all down in their necks; and even though by the time I left I knew where all the stories came from and where they were going, I was never bored, never even unsurprised. Obviously, what they really wanted to tell you was how tired they were and how sick of it, how moved they'd been and how afraid. But maybe that was me, by then my posture was shot: "reporter." ("Must be pretty hard to stay detached," a man on the plane to San Francisco said, and I said, "Impossible.") After a year I felt so plugged in to all the stories and the images and the fear that even the dead started telling me stories, you'd hear them out of a remote but accessible space where there were no ideas, no emotions, no facts, no proper language, only clean information. However many times it happened, whether I'd known them or not, no matter what I'd felt about them or the way they'd died, their story was always there and it was always the same: it went, "Put yourself in my place."

One afternoon I mistook a bloody nose for a head-wound, and I didn't have to wonder anymore how I'd behave if I ever got hit. We were walking out on a sweep north of Tay Ninh City, toward the Cambodian border, and a mortar round came in about thirty yards away. I had no sense of those distances then, even after six or seven weeks in

with again), one was on his hands and knees vomiting some evil pink substance, and one, quite near us, was propped up against a tree facing away from the direction of the round, making himself look at the incredible thing that had just happened to his leg, screwed around about once at some point below his knee like a goofy scarecrow leg. He looked away and then back again, looking at it for a few seconds longer each time, then he settled in for about a minute, shaking his head and smiling, until his face became serious and he passed out.

By then I'd found my nose and realized what had happened, all that had happened, not even broken, my glasses weren't even broken. I took the kid's canteen and soaked my sweat scarf, washing the blood off where it had caked on my lip and chin. He had stopped apologizing, and there was no pity in his face anymore. When I handed his canteen back to him, he was laughing at me.

I never told that story to anyone, and I never went back to that outfit again either.

III

In Saigon I always went to sleep stoned so I almost always lost my dreams, probably just as well, sock in deep and dim under that information and get whatever rest you could, wake up tapped of all images but the ones remembered from the day or the week before, with only the taste of a bad dream in your mouth like you'd been chewing on a roll of dirty old pennies in your sleep. I'd watched grunts asleep putting out the REM's like a firefight in the dark, I'm sure it was the same with me. They'd say (I'd ask) that they didn't remember

before my feet even hit the floor. Dear Mom, stoned again.

In the Highlands, where the Montagnards would trade you a pound of legendary grass for a carton of Salems, I got stoned with some infantry from the 4th. One of them had worked for months on his pipe, beautifully carved and painted with flowers and peace symbols. There was a reedy little man in the circle who grinned all the time but hardly spoke. He pulled a thick plastic bag out of his pack and handed it over to me. It was full of what looked like large pieces of dried fruit. I was stoned and hungry, I almost put my hand in there, but it had a bad weight to it. The other men were giving each other looks, some amused, some embarrassed and even angry. Someone had told me once, there were a lot more ears than heads in Vietnam; just information. When I handed it back he was still grinning, but he looked sadder than a monkey.

In Saigon and Danang we'd get stoned together and keep the common pool stocked and tended. It was bottomless and alive with Lurps, seals, recondos, Green-Beret bushmasters, redundant mutilators, heavy rapers, eye-shooters, widow-makers, nametakers, classic essential American types; point men, *isolatos* and outriders like they were programmed in their genes to do it, the first taste made them crazy for it, just like they knew it would. You thought you were separate and protected, you could travel the war for a hundred years, a swim in that pool could still be worth a piece of your balance.

We'd all heard about the man in the Highlands was was "building his own gook," parts were the least of his troubles. In Chu Lai some Marines pointed a man out to me and swore to God they'd seen him bayonet a wounded NVA and then lick

Corps, he hadn't said a word about what had gone on up there. "Spaced": he was sitting on the floor by the air-conditioner with his back against the wall trying to watch the sweat running down from his hairline.

We were all in a room at the Continental Hotel that belonged to Keith Kay, the CBS cameraman. It was early May and there was a lot of heavy combat all around the city, a big offensive, friends came in from there and went out again all week long. Across the way, on the latticed porches of the Continental annex, we could see the Indians shuffle back and forth in their underwear, bushed from another hard day of buying and selling money. (Their mosque, near L'Amiral Restaurant, was called the Bank of India. When the Saigon police, the White Mice, raided it they found two million in cold green.) There were trucks and jeeps and a thousand bikes moving in the street, and a little girl with a withered leg darting back and forth on wooden crutches faster than a dragonfly to sell her cigarettes. She had a face like a child dakini, so beautiful that people who needed to keep their edge blunt could hardly bear to look at her. Her competition were street boys, "Changee money," "Boom-boom picture," "Dinkydao cigarette," hustle and connection ran like a current down Tu Do, from the cathedral to the river. Rounding Le Loi there was a large group of correspondents coming back from the briefing, standard diurnal informational freak-o-rama, Five O'Clock Follies, Jive at Five, war stories; at the corner they broke formation and went to their offices to file, we watched them, the wasted clocking the wasted.

A new correspondent came into the room to say hello, just arrived from New York, and he started asking Dana a lot of questions right away, sort of

through his spine straight to the old pleasure center in his cream-cheese brain, shaking his head so that his hair waved all around him, Have You Ever Been Experienced?

"What does it look like when a man gets hit in the balls?" the new man said, as though that was the question he'd really meant to ask all along, and it came as close as you could get to a breach of taste in that room; palpable embarrassment all around, Flynn moved his eyes like he was following a butterfly up out of sight, Page got sniffy and offended, but he was amused, too. Dana just sat there putting out the still rays, taking snaps with his eyes. "Oh I dunno," he said. "It all just goes sort of gooey."

We all started to laugh, everyone except Dana, because he'd seen that, he was just telling the man. I didn't hear what the man started to ask next, but Dana stopped him and said, "Only thing I can tell you that might actually do you some good is to go back up to your room and practice hitting the floor for a while."

Beautiful for once and only once, just past dawn flying towards the center of the city in a Loach, view from a bubble floating at 800 feet. In that space, at that hour, you could see what people had seen forty years before, Paris of the East, Pearl of the Orient, long open avenues lined and bowered over by trees running into spacious parks, precisioned scale, all under the soft shell from a million breakfast fires, camphor smoke rising and diffusing, covering Saigon and the shining veins of the river with a warmth like the return of better times. Just a projection, that was the thing about chopper, you had to come down sometime, down

editions of Proust, Malraux, Camus. One of them talked to me a few times but we couldn't really communicate, all I understood was his obsessive comparison between Rome and Washington, and that he seemed to believe that Poe had been a French writer. In the late afternoon the Cowboys would leave the cafés and milk bars and ride down hard on Lam Son Square to pick the Allies. They could snap a Rolex off your wrist like a hawk hitting a field mouse; wallets, pens, cameras, eye-glasses, anything; if the war had gone on any longer they'd have found a way to whip the boots off your feet. They'd hardly leave their saddles and they never looked back. There was a soldier down from the 1st Division who was taking snap-shots of his friends with some bar girls in front of the Vietnamese National Assembly. He'd gotten his shot focused and centered but before he pushed the button his camera was a block away, leaving him in the bike's backwash with a fresh pink welt on his throat where the cord had been torn and helpless amazement on his face, "Well I'll be dipped in shit!"; as a little boy raced across the square, zipped a piece of cardboard up the soldier's shirt-front and took off around the corner with his Paper Mate. The White Mice stood around gig-gling, but there were a lot of us watching from the Continental terrace, a kind of gasp went up from the tables, and later when he came up for a beer he said, "I'm goin' back to the war, man, this fucking Saigon is too much for me." There was a large group of civilian engineers there, the same men you'd see in the restaurants throwing food at each other, and one of them, a fat old boy, said, "You ever catch one of them li'l nigs just pinch 'em. Pinch 'em hard. Boy, they hate that."

Five to seven were bleary low hours in Saigon,

her as "beautiful," but I don't know how anybody knew that. The commander of one of the Saigon MP battalions said he thought it was a man dressed in an *ao dai* because a .45 was "an awful lot of gun for a itty bitty Vietnamese woman."

Saigon, the center, where every action in the bushes hundreds of miles away fed back into town on a karmic wire strung so tight that if you touched it in the early morning it would sing all day and all night. Nothing so horrible ever happened up-country that it was beyond language fix and press relations, a squeeze fit into the computers would make the heaviest numbers jump up and dance. You'd either meet an optimism that no violence could unconvince or a cynicism that would eat itself empty every day and then turn, hungry and malignant, on whatever it could for a bite, friendly or hostile, it didn't matter. Those men called dead Vietnamese "believers," a lost American platoon was "a black eye," they talked as though killing a man was nothing more than depriving him of his vigor.

It seemed the least of the war's contradictions that to lose your worst sense of American shame you had to leave the Dial Soapers in Saigon and a hundred headquarters who spoke goodworks and killed nobody themselves, and go out to the grungy men in the jungle who talked bloody murder and killed people all the time. It was true that the grunts stripped belts and packs and weapons from their enemies; Saigon wasn't a flat market, these goods filtered down and in with the other spoils: Rolexes, cameras, snakeskin shoes from Taiwan, air-brush portraits of nude Vietnamese women with breasts like varnished beach balls, huge wooden carvings that they set on their desks to give you the finger when you walked into their

times, no bearings and none in sight, thinking, *Where the fuck am I?*, fallen into some unnatural East-West interface, a California corridor cut and bought and burned deep into Asia, and once we'd done it we couldn't remember what for. It was axiomatic that it was about ideological space, we were there to bring them the choice, bringing it to them like Sherman bringing the Jubilee through Georgia, clean through it, wall to wall with pacified indigenous and scorched earth. (In the Vietnamese sawmills they had to change the blades every five minutes, some of our lumber had gotten into some of theirs.) There was such a dense concentration of American energy there, American and essentially adolescent, if that energy could have been channeled into anything more than noise, waste and pain it would have lighted up Indochina for a thousand years.

The Mission and the motion: military arms and civilian arms, more combatant between themselves than together against the Cong. Gun arms, knife arms, pencil arms, head-and-stomach arms, hearts-and-minds arms, flying arms, creeping-peeping arms, information arms as tricky as the arms of Plastic Man. At the bottom was the shitface grunt, at the top a Command trinity: a blue-eyed, hero-faced general, a geriatrics-emergency ambassador and a hale, heartless CIA performer. (Robert "Blowtorch" Komer, chief of COORDS, spook anagram for Other War, pacification, another word for war. If William Blake had "reported" to him that he'd seen angels in the trees, Komer would have tried to talk him out of it. Failing there, he'd have ordered defoliation.) All through the middle were the Vietnam War and the Vietnamese, not always exactly innocent bystanders, probably no accident that we'd found each other. If milk snakes could

on street corners. Deep in the alleys you could hear small Buddhist chimes ringing for peace, *hoa bien;* smell incense in the middle of the thickest Asian street funk; see groups of ARVN with their families waiting for transport huddled around a burning prayer strip. Sermonettes came over Armed Forces radio every couple of hours, once I heard a chaplain from the 9th Division starting up, "Oh Gawd, help us learn to live with Thee in a more dynamic way in these perilous times, that we may better serve Thee in the struggle against Thine enemies. . . ." Holy war, long-nose jihad like a face-off between one god who would hold the coonskin to the wall while we nailed it up, and another whose detachment would see the blood run out of ten generations, if that was how long it took for the wheel to go around.

And around. While the last falling-off contacts were still going on and the last casualties being dusted off, Command added Dak To to our victory list, a reflexive move supported by the Saigon press corps but never once or for a minute by reporters who'd seen it going on from meters or even inches away, and this latest media defection added more bitterness to an already rotten mix, leaving the commanding general of the 4th to wonder out loud and in my hearing whether we were or weren't all Americans in this thing together. I said I thought we were. For sure we were.

". . . Wow I love it in the movies when they say like, 'Okay Jim, where do you want it?'"

"Right! Right! Yeah, beautiful, I don't want it at all! Haw, shit . . . where do you fucking want it?"

Mythopathic moment; *Fort Apache,* where Henry Fonda as the new colonel says to John Wayne, the old hand, "We saw some Apache as

and said, "What does that asshole know about tunnels?")

A few months earlier there had been an attempt Higher to crank up the Home For Christmas rumor, but it wouldn't take, the troop consensus was too strong, it went, "Never happen." If a commander told you he thought he had it pretty well under control it was like talking to a pessimist. Most would say that they either had it wrapped up or wound down; "He's all pissed out, Charlie's all pissed out, booger's shot his whole wad," one of them promised me, while in Saigon it would be restructured for briefings, "He no longer maintains in our view capability to mount, execute or sustain a serious offensive action," and a reporter behind me, from *The New York Times* no less, laughed and said, "Mount this Colonel." But in the boonies, where they were deprived of all information except what they'd gathered for themselves on either side of the treeline, they'd look around like someone was watching and say, "I dunno, Charlie's up to something. Slick, slick, that fucker's *so* slick. Watch!"

The summer before, thousands of Marines had gone humping across northern I Corps in multi-division sweeps, "Taking the D out of DMZ," but the North never really broke out into the open for it, hard to believe that anyone ever thought that they would. Mostly it was an invasion of a thousand operation-miles of high summer dry season stroke weather, six-canteen patrols that came back either contactless or chewed over by ambushes and quick, deft mortar-rocket attacks, some from other Marine outfits. By September they were "containing" at Con Thien, sitting there while the NVA killed them with artillery. In II Corps a month of random contact near the Laotian border had sharp-

going off? Mission intellectuals like 1954 as the reference date; if you saw as far back as War II and the Japanese occupation you were practically a historical visionary. "Realists" said that it began for us in 1961, and the common run of Mission flack insisted on 1965, post-Tonkin Resolution, as though all the killing that had gone before wasn't really war. Anyway, you couldn't use standard methods to date the doom; might as well say that Vietnam was where the Trail of Tears was headed all along, the turnaround point where it would touch and come back to form a containing perimeter; might just as well lay it on the proto-Gringos who found the New England woods too raw and empty for their peace and filled them up with their own imported devils. Maybe it was already over for us in Indochina when Alden Pyle's body washed up under the bridge at Dakao, his lungs all full of mud; maybe it caved in with Dien Bien Phu. But the first happened in a novel, and while the second happened on the ground it happened to the French, and Washington gave it no more substance than if Graham Greene had made it up too. Straight history, auto-revised history, history without handles, for all the books and articles and white papers, all the talk and the miles of film, something wasn't answered, it wasn't even asked. We were backgrounded, deep, but when the background started sliding forward not a single life was saved by the information. The thing had transmitted too much energy, it heated up too hot, hiding low under the fact-figure crossfire there was a secret history, and not a lot of people felt like running in there to bring it out.

One day in 1963 Henry Cabot Lodge was walking around the Saigon Zoo with some reporters, and a tiger pissed on him through the bars of its

were dead. There were executive spooks who'd turn up at airstrips and jungle clearings sweating like a wheel of cheese in their white suits and neckties; bureau spooks who sat on dead asses in Dalat and Qui Nhon, or out jerking off in some New Life Village; Air America spooks who could take guns or junk or any kind of death at all and make it fly; Special Forces spooks running around in a fury of skill to ice Victor Charlie.

History's heavy attrition, tic and toc with teeth, the smarter ones saw it winding down for them on the day that Lodge first arrived in Saigon and commandeered the villa of the current CIA chief, a moment of history that seemed even sweeter when you knew that the villa had once been headquarters of the Deuxième Bureau. Officially, the complexion of the problem had changed (too many people were getting killed, for one thing), and the romance of spooking started to fall away like dead meat from a bone. As sure as heat rises, their time was over. The war passed along, this time into the hard hands of firepower freaks out to eat the country whole, and with no fine touches either, leaving the spooks on the beach.

They never became as dangerous as they'd wanted to be, they never knew how dangerous they really were. Their adventure became our war, then a war bogged down in time, so much time so badly accounted for that it finally became entrenched as an institution because there had never been room made for it to go anywhere else. The Irregulars either got out or became regular in a hurry. By 1967 all you saw was the impaired spook reflex, prim adventurers living too long on the bloodless fringes of the action, heartbroken and memory-ruptured, working alone together toward a classified universe. They seemed like the saddest casualties

could even put you on the approach to clairaudience. You thought you heard impossible things: damp roots breathing, fruit sweating, fervid bug action, the heartbeat of tiny animals.

You could sustain that sensitivity for a long time, either until the babbling and chittering and shrieking of the jungle had started up again, or until something familiar brought you out of it, a helicopter flying around above your canopy or the strangely reassuring sound next to you of one going into the chamber. Once we heard a really frightening thing blaring down from a Psyops soundship broadcasting the sound of a baby crying. You wouldn't have wanted to hear that during daylight, let alone at night when the volume and distortion came down through two or three layers of cover and froze us all in place for a moment. And there wasn't much release in the pitched hysteria of the message that followed, hyper-Vietnamese like an icepick in the ear, something like, "Friendly Baby, GVN Baby, Don't Let This Happen to *Your* Baby, Resist the Viet Cong Today!"

Sometimes you'd get so tired that you'd forget where you were and sleep the way you hadn't slept since you were a child. I know that a lot of people there never got up from that kind of sleep; some called them lucky (Never knew what hit him), some called them fucked (If he'd been on the stick . . .), but that was worse than academic, everyone's death got talked about, it was a way of constantly touching and turning the odds, and real sleep was at a premium. (I met a ranger-recondo who could go to sleep just like that, say, "Guess I'll get some," close his eyes and be there, day or night, sitting or lying down, sleeping through some things but not others; a loud radio or a 105 firing outside the tent wouldn't wake him, but a rustle in

observe. Imagine being too tired to snap a flak jacket closed, too tired to clean your rifle, too tired to guard a light, too tired to deal with the half-inch margins of safety that moving through the war often demanded, just too tired to give a fuck and then dying behind that exhaustion. There were times when the whole war itself seemed tapped of its vitality: epic enervation, the machine running half-assed and depressed, fueled on the watery residue of last year's war-making energy. Entire divisions would function in a bad dream state, acting out a weird set of moves without any connection to their source. Once I talked for maybe five minutes with a sergeant who had just brought his squad in from a long patrol before I realized that the dopey-dummy film over his eyes and the fly abstraction of his words were coming from deep sleep. He was standing there at the bar of the NCO club with his eyes open and a beer in his hand, responding to some dream conversation far inside his head. It really gave me the creeps—this was the second day of the Tet Offensive, our installation was more or less surrounded, the only secure road out of there was littered with dead Vietnamese, information was scarce and I was pretty touchy and tired myself—and for a second I imagined that I was talking to a dead man. When I told him about it later he just laughed and said, "Shit, that's nothing. I do that all the time."

One night I woke up and heard the sounds of a firefight going on kilometers away, a "skirmish" outside our perimeter, muffled by distance to sound like the noises we made playing guns as children, KSSSHH KSSSHH; we knew it was more authentic than BANG BANG, it enriched the game and this game was the same, only way out of hand at last,

at its pitiless discretion. All you could say that wasn't fundamentally lame was something like, "He who bites it this day is safe from the next," and that was exactly what nobody wanted to hear.

After enough time passed and memory receded and settled, the name itself became a prayer, coded like all prayer to go past the extremes of petition and gratitude: Vietnam Vietnam Vietnam, say again, until the word lost all its old loads of pain, pleasure, horror, guilt, nostalgia. Then and there, everyone was just trying to get through it, existential crunch, no atheists in foxholes like you wouldn't believe. Even bitter refracted faith was better than none at all, like the black Marine I'd heard about during the heavy shelling at Con Thien who said, "Don't worry, baby, God'll think of something."

Flip religion, it was so far out, you couldn't blame anybody for believing anything. Guys dressed up in Batman fetishes, I saw a whole squad like that, it gave them a kind of dumb esprit. Guys stuck the ace of spades in their helmet bands, they picked relics off of an enemy they'd killed, a little transfer of power; they carried around five-pound Bibles from home, crosses, St. Christophers, mezuzahs, locks of hair, girlfriends' underwear, snaps of their families, their wives, their dogs, their cows, their cars, pictures of John Kennedy, Lyndon Johnson, Martin Luther King, Huey Newton, the Pope, Che Guevara, the Beatles, Jimi Hendrix, wiggier than cargo cultists. One man was carrying an oatmeal cookie through his tour, wrapped up in foil and plastic and three pair of socks. He took a lot of shit about it. ("When you go to sleep we're gonna eat your fucking cookie"), but his wife had baked it and mailed it to him, he wasn't kidding.

On operations you'd see men clustering around the charmed grunt that many outfits created who

possession of the madness that had been waiting there in trust for them for eigheen or twenty-five or fifty years. Every time there was combat you had a license to go maniac, everyone snapped over the line at least once there and nobody noticed, they hardly noticed if you forgot to snap back again.

One afternoon at Khe Sanh a Marine opened the door of a latrine and was killed by a grenade that had been rigged on the door. The Command tried to blame it on a North Vietnamese infiltrator, but the grunts knew what had happened: "Like a gook is really gonna tunnel all the way in here to booby-trap a shithouse, right? Some guy just flipped out is all." And it became another one of those stories that moved across the DMZ, making people laugh and shake their heads and look knowingly at each other, but shocking no one. They'd talk about physical wounds in one way and psychic wounds in another, each man in a squad would tell you how crazy everyone else in the squad was, everyone knew grunts who'd gone crazy in the middle of a firefight, gone crazy on patrol, gone crazy back at camp, gone crazy on R&R, gone crazy during their first month home. Going crazy was built into the tour, the best you could hope for was that it didn't happen around you, the kind of crazy that made men empty clips into strangers or fix grenades on latrine doors. That was *really* crazy; anything less was almost standard, as standard as the vague prolonged stares and involuntary smiles, common as ponchos or 16's or any other piece of war issue. If you wanted someone to know you'd gone insane you really had to sound off like you had a pair, "Scream a lot, and all the time."

Some people just wanted to blow it all to hell, animal vegetable and mineral. They wanted a Viet-

a Dove or a Hawk?" and "Would you rather fight them here or in Pasadena?" *Maybe we could beat them in Pasadena,* I'd think, but I wouldn't say it, especially not here where they knew that I knew that they really weren't fighting anybody anywhere anyway, it made them pretty touchy. That night I listened while a colonel explained the war in terms of protein. We were a nation of high-protein, meat-eating hunters, while the other guy just ate rice and a few grungy fish heads. We were going to club him to death with out meat; what could you say except, "Colonel, you're insane"? It was like turning up in the middle of some black looneytune where the Duck had all the lines. I only jumped in once, spontaneous as shock, during Tet when I heard a doctor bragging that he'd refused to allow wounded Vietnamese into his ward. "But Jesus Christ," I said, "didn't you take the Hippocratic Oath?" but he was ready for me. "Yeah," he said, "I took it in America." Doomsday celebs, techno-maniac projectionists; chemicals, gases, lasers, sonic-electric ballbreakers that were still on the boards; and for back-up, deep in all their hearts, there were always the Nukes, they loved to remind you that we had some, "right here in-country." Once I met a colonel who had a plan to shorten the war by dropping piranha into the paddies of the North. He was talking fish but his dreamy eyes were full of mega-death.

"Come on," the captain said, "we'll take you out to play Cowboys and Indians." We walked out from Song Be in a long line, maybe a hundred men; rifles, heavy automatics, mortars, portable one-shot rocket-launchers, radios, medics; breaking into some kind of sweep formation, five files with small teams of specialists in each file. A gunship flew close

hunting," a platoon leader told me. "Me and my father and my brothers used to make a hundred a year between us maybe. I swear to God, I never saw anything like this."

Who had? Nothing like it ever when we caught a bunch of them out in the open and close together, we really ripped it then, volatile piss-off, crazed expenditure, Godzilla never drew that kind of fire. We even had a small language for our fire: "discreet burst," "probe," "prime selection," "constructive load," but I never saw it as various, just compulsive eruption, the Mad Minute for an hour. Charles really wrote the book on fire control, putting one round into the heart of things where fifty of ours might go and still not hit anything. Sometimes we put out so much fire you couldn't tell whether any of it was coming back or not. When it was, it filled your ears and your head until you thought you were hearing it with your stomach. An English correspondent I knew made a cassette of one of the heavy ones, he said he used it to seduce American girls.

Sometimes you felt too thin and didn't want to get into anything at all and it would land on you like your next-to-last breath. Sometimes your chops for action and your terror would reach a different balance and you'd go looking for it everywhere, and nothing would happen, except a fire ant would fly up your nose or you'd grow a crotch rot or you'd lie awake all night waiting for morning so you could get up and wait on your feet. Whichever way it went, you were covering the war, your choice of story told it all and in Vietnam an infatuation like that with violence wouldn't go unrequited for very long, it would come and put its wild mouth all over you.

"Quakin' and Shakin'," they called it, great balls

Phu Bai one last shell came in, landing in the middle of a pile of full body bags, making a mess that no one wanted to clean up, "a real shit detail." It was after midnight when I finally got back to Saigon, riding in from Tan Son Nhut in an open jeep with some sniper-obsessed MP's, and there was a small package of mail waiting for me at the hotel. I put my fatigues out in the hall room and closed the door on them. I may have even locked it. I had the I Corps DT's, livers, spleens, brains, a blue-black swollen thumb moved around and flashed to me, they were playing over the walls of the shower where I spent a half-hour, they were on the bedsheets, but I wasn't afraid of them, I was laughing at them, what could they do to me? I filled a water glass with Armagnac and rolled a joint, and then I started to read my mail. In one of the letters there was news that a friend of mine had killed himself in New York. When I turned off the lights and got into bed I lay there trying to remember what he had looked like. He had done it with pills, but no matter what I tried to imagine, all I saw was blood and bone fragment, not my dead friend. After a while I broke through for a second and saw him, but by that time all I could do with it was file him in with the rest and go to sleep.

Between what contact did to you and how tired you got, between the farout things you saw or heard and what you personally lost out of all that got blown away, the war made a place for you that was all yours. Finding it was like listening to esoteric music, you didn't hear it in any essential way through all the repetitions until your own breath had entered it and become another instrument, and by then it wasn't just music anymore, it was experience. Life-as-movie, war-as-(war) movie, war-

in there before you could swallow, turn your breath fouler than corpse gas. There were times when your fear would take directions so wild that you had to stop and watch the spin. Forget the Cong, the *trees* would kill you, the elephant grass grew up homicidal, the ground you were walking over possessed malignant intelligence, your whole environment was a bath. Even so, considering where you were and what was happening to so many people, it was a privilege just to be able to feel afraid.

So you learned about fear, it was hard to know what you really learned about courage. How many times did somebody have to run in front of a machine gun before it became an act of cowardice? What about those acts that didn't require courage to perform, but made you a coward if you didn't? It was hard to know at the moment, easy to make a mistake when it came, like the mistake of thinking that all you needed to perform a witness act were your eyes. A lot of what people called courage was only undifferentiated energy cut loose by the intensity of the moment, mind loss that sent the actor on an incredible run; if he survived it he had the chance later to decide whether he'd really been brave or just overcome with life, even ecstasy. A lot of people found the guts to just call it all off and refuse to ever go out anymore, they turned and submitted to the penalty end of the system or they just split. A lot of reporters, too, I had friends in the press corps who went out once or twice and then never again. Sometimes I thought that they were the sanest, most serious people of all, although to be honest I never said so until my time there was almost over.

"We had this gook and we was gonna skin him"

strip in Can Tho with a .30-caliber automatic in my hands, firing cover for a four-man reaction team trying to get back in. One last war story.

The first night of the Tet Offensive we were in the Special Forces C Camp for the Delta, surrounded, as far as we knew, and with nothing but bad news filtering in: from Hue, from Danang, from Qui Nhon, from Khe Sanh, from Ban Me Thuot, from Saigon itself, "lost" as we understood it at the moment, they had the embassy, they had Cholon, Tan Son Nhut was burning, we were in the Alamo, no place else, and I wasn't a reporter, I was a shooter.

In the morning there were about a dozen dead Vietnamese across the field there where we'd been firing. We sent a truck over to load them on and get them away. It all happened so fast, as they say, as everyone who has ever been through it has always said; we were sitting around smoking grass and listening to what we thought were Tet fireworks coming from the town, and then coming closer until we weren't stoned anymore, until the whole night had passed and I was looking at the empty clips around my feet behind the berm, telling myself that there would never be any way to know for sure. I couldn't remember ever feeling so tired, so changed, so happy.

Thousands of people died in Vietnam that night, the twelve across the field, a hundred more along the road between the camp and the Can Tho hospital compound where I worked all the next day, not a reporter or a shooter but a medic, unskilled and scared. When we got back to the camp that night I threw away the fatigues I'd been wearing. And for the next six years I saw them all, the ones I'd really seen and the ones I'd imagined, theirs and ours, friends I'd loved and strangers,

Hell Sucks

During the first weeks of the Tet Offensive the curfew began early in the afternoon and was strictly enforced. By 2:30 each day Saigon looked like the final reel of *On the Beach*, a desolate city whose long avenues held nothing but refuse, windblown papers, small distinct piles of human excrement and the dead flowers and spent firecracker casings of the Lunar New Year. Alive, Saigon had been depressing enough, but during the Offensive it became so stark that, in an odd way, it was invigorating. The trees along the main streets looked like they'd been struck by lightning, and it became unusually, uncomfortably cold, one more piece of freak luck in a place where nothing was in its season. With so much filth growing in so many streets and alleys, an epidemic of plague was feared, and if there was ever a place that suggested plague, demanded it, it was Saigon in the Emergency. American civilians, engineers and construction workers who were making it here like they'd never made it at home began forming into large armed bands, carrying .45's and grease guns and Swedish K's, and no mob of hysterical vigilantes ever promised more bad news. You'd see them at ten in the morning on the terrace of the Continental waiting for the bar to open, barely able to light their own cigarettes until it did. The crowds on Tu Do Street looked like Ensor processioners, and there was a corruption in the air that had nothing to do with government workers on the take. After seven in

British correspondent compared the Mission posture to the captain of the *Titanic* announcing, "There's no cause for alarm, we're only stopping briefly to take on a little ice."

By the time I got back to Saigon on the fourth day a lot of information from around the country had settled, and it was bad, even after you picked out the threads of rumor: like the one about the "Caucasians," obviously Americans, fighting for the VC, or the one about thousands of NVA executions in Hue and the "shallow graves" in the flats outside the city, both of which proved true. Almost as much as the grunts and the Vietnamese, Tet was pushing correspondents closer to the wall than they'd ever wanted to go. I realized later that, however childish I might remain, actual youth had been pressed out of me in just the three days that it took me to cross the sixty miles between Can Tho and Saigon. In Saigon, I saw friends flipping out almost completely; a few left, some took to their beds for days with the exhaustion of deep depression. I went the other way, hyper and agitated, until I was only doing three hours of sleep a night. A friend on the *Times* said he didn't mind his nightmares so much as the waking impulse to file on them. An old-timer who'd covered war since the Thirties heard us pissing and moaning about how *terrible* it was and he snorted, "Ha, I love you guys. You guys are beautiful. What the fuck did you think it was?" We thought it was already past the cut-off point where every war is just like every other war; if we knew how rough it was going to get, we might have felt better. After a few days the air routes opened again, and we went up to Hue.

Going in there were sixty of us packed into a

city ground. (In Hue he turned out to be incredibly valuable. I saw him pouring out about a hundred rounds of .30-caliber fire into a breach in the wall, laughing, "You got to bring some to get some"; he seemed to be about the only man in Delta Company who hadn't been hurt yet.) And there was a Marine correspondent, Sergeant Dale Dye, who sat with a tall yellow flower sticking out of his helmet cover, a really outstanding target. He was rolling his eyes around and saying, "Oh yes, oh yes, Charlie's got his shit together here, this will be *bad,*" and smiling happily. It was the same smile I saw a week later when a sniper's bullet tore up a wall two inches above his head, odd cause for amusement in anyone but a grunt.

Everyone else in the truck had that wild haunted going-West look that said it was perfectly correct to be here where the fighting would be the worst, where you wouldn't have half of what you needed, where it was colder than Nam ever got. On their helmets and flak jackets they'd written the names of old operations, of girlfriends, their war names (FAR FROM FEARLESS, MICKEY'S MONKEY, AVENGER V, SHORT TIME SAFETY MOE), their fantasies (BORN TO LOSE, BORN TO RAISE HELL, BORN TO DIE), their ongoing information (HELL SUCKS, TIME IS ON MY SIDE, JUST YOU AND ME GOD—RIGHT?). One kid called to me, "Hey man! You want a story, man? Here man, write this: I'm up there on 881, this was May, I'm just up there walkin' the ridgeline like a move star and this Zip jumps up smack into me, lays his AK-47 fucking right *into* me, only he's so *amazed* at my *cool* I got my whole clip off 'fore he knew how to thank me for it. Grease one." After twenty kilometers of this, in spite of the black roiling sky ahead, we could

villas of officials and the French-architected University buildings. Many of those villas had been destroyed and much of the University permanently damaged. In the middle of the street a couple of ambulances from the German Mission had been blown up, and the Cercle Sportif was covered with bullet holes and shrapnel. The rain had brought up the green, it stretched out cased in thick white fog. In the park itself, four fat green dead lay sprawled around a tall, ornate cage, inside of which sat a small, shivering monkey. One of the correspondents along stepped over the corpses to feed it some fruit. (Days later, I came back to the spot. The corpses were gone, but so was the monkey. There had been so many refugees and so little food then, and someone must have eaten him.) The Marines of 2/5 had secured almost all of the central south bank and were now fanning out to the west, fighting and clearing one of the major canals. We were waiting for some decision on whether or not U.S. Marines would be going into the Citadel itself, but no one had any doubts about what that decision would be. We sat there taking in the dread by watching the columns of smoke across the river, receiving occasional sniper rounds, infrequent bursts of .50-caliber, watching the Navy LCU's on the river getting shelled from the wall. One Marine next to me was saying that it was just a damned shame, all them poor people, all them nice-looking houses, they even had a Shell station there. He was looking at the black napalm blasts and the wreckage along the wall. "Looks like the Imperial City's had the schnitz," he said.

The courtyard of the American compound in Hue was filled with puddles from the rain, and the canvas tops of the jeeps and trucks sagged with the

they'd started the fire to cover an escape. The ARVN and a few Americans were shooting blindly into the flames, and the bodies were burning where they fell. Civilian dead lay out on the sidewalks only a block from the compound, and the park by the river was littered with dead. It was cold and the sun never came out once, but the rain did things to the corpses that were worse in their way than anything the sun could have done. It was on one of those days that I realized that the only corpse I couldn't bear to look at would be the one I would never have to see.

It stayed cold and dark like that for the next ten days, and that damp gloom was the background for all the footage that we took out of the Citadel. What little sunlight there was caught the heavy motes of dust that blew up from the wreckage of the east wall, held it until everything you saw was filtered through it. And you saw things from unaccustomed angles, quick looks from a running crouch, or up from flat out, hearing the hard dry rattle of shrapnel scudding against the debris around you. With all of that dust blowing around, the acrid smell of cordite would hang in the air for a long time after firefights, and there was the CS gas that we'd fired at the NVA blowing back in over our positions. It was impossible to get a clean breath with all of that happening, and there was that other smell too that came up from the shattered heaps of stone wherever an airstrike had come in. It held to the lining of your nostrils and worked itself into the weave of your fatigues, and weeks later, miles away, you'd wake up at night and it would be in the room with you. The NVA had dug themselves so deeply into the wall that airstrikes had to open it meter by meter, dropping

through it alive. A despair set in among members of the battalion that the older ones, the veterans of two other wars, had never seen before. Once or twice, when the men from Graves Registration took the personal effects from the packs and pockets of dead Marines, they found letters from home that had been delivered days before and were still unopened.

We were running some wounded onto the back of a half-ton truck, and one of the young Marines kept crying from his stretcher. His sergeant held both of his hands, and the Marine kept saying, "Shit, Sarge, I ain' gone make it. Oh damn, I'm gone die, ain't I?" "No you ain't gonna die, for Christ's sake," the sergeant said. "Oh yeah, Sarge, yeah, I am." "Crowley," the sergeant said, "you ain't hurt that bad. I want you to just shut the fuck up. You ain't done a thing except bitch ever since we got to this fucking Hue City." But the sergeant didn't really know. The kid had been hit in the throat, and you couldn't tell about those. Throat wounds were bad. Everyone was afraid of throat wounds.

We lucked out on our connections. At the battalion aid station we got a chopper that carried us and a dozen dead Marines to the base at Phu Bai, and three minutes after we landed there we caught a C-130 to Danang. Hitching in from the airfield, we found a Psyops officer who felt sorry for us and drove us all the way to the press center. As we came in the gate we could see that the net was up and the daily volleyball game between the Marines assigned to the press center was on.

"Where the hell have *you* guys been?" one of them asked. We looked pretty fucked up.

The inside of the dining room was freezing with air-conditioning. I sat at a table and ordered a ham-

At night in the CP, the major who commanded the battalion would sit reading his maps, staring vacantly at the trapezoid of the Citadel. It could have been a scene in a Norman farmhouse twenty-five years ago, with candles burning on the tables, bottles of red wine arranged along damaged shelves, the chill in the room, the high ceilings, the heavy ornate cross on the wall. The major had not slept for five nights, and for the fifth night in a row he assured us that tomorrow would get it for sure, the final stretch of wall would be taken and he had all the Marines he needed to do it. And one of his aides, a tough mustang first lieutenant, would pitch a hard, ironic smile above the major's stare, a smile that rejected good news, it was like hearing him say, "The major here is full of shit, and we both know it."

Sometimes a company would find itself completely cut off, and it would take hours for the Marines to get their wounded out. I remember one Marine with a headwound who finally made it to the Battalion CP when the jeep he was in stalled. He finally jumped out and started to push, knowing it was the only way out of there. Most of the tanks and trucks that carried casualties had to move up a long straight road without cover, and they began calling it Rocket Alley. Every tank the Marines had there had been hit at least once. An epiphany of Hue appeared in John Olson's great photograph for *Life*, the wounded from Delta Company hurriedly piled on a tank. Sometimes, on the way to the aid station the more seriously wounded would take on that bad color, the gray-blue fishbelly promise of death that would spread upward from the chest and cover the face. There was one Marine who had been shot through the neck, and all the way out the corpsmen massaged his chest. By the

almost every casualty, remember conversations we'd had days or even hours earlier, and that's when I left, riding a medevac with a lieutenant who was covered with blood-soaked bandages. He'd been hit in both legs, both arms, the chest and head, his ears and eyes were full of caked blood, and he asked a photographer in the chopper to get a picture of him like this to send to his wife.

But by then the battle for Hue was almost over. The Cav was working the northwest corner of the Citadel, and elements of the 101st had come in through what had formerly been an NVA re-supply route. (In five days these outfits lost as many men as the Marines had in three weeks.) Vietnamese Marines and some of the 1st ARVN Division had been moving the remaining NVA down toward the wall. The NVA flag that had flown for so long over the south wall had been cut down, and in its place an American flag had been put up. Two days later the Hoc Bao, Vietnamese Rangers, stormed through the walls of the Imperial Palace, but there were no NVA left inside. Except for a few bodies in the moat, most of their dead had been buried. When they'd first come into Hue the NVA had sat at banquets given for them by the people. Before they left, they'd skimmed all the edible vegetation from the surface of the moat. Seventy percent of Vietnam's one lovely city was destroyed, and if the landscape seemed desolate, imagine how the figures in that landscape looked.

There were two official ceremonies marking the expulsion of the NVA, both flag-raisings. On the south bank of the Perfume River, 200 refugees from one of the camps were recruited to stand, sullen and silent in the rain, and watch the GVN flag being run up. But the rope snapped, and the crowd, thinking the VC had shot it down, broke

everything. The crown of the main gate had collapsed, and in the garden the broken branches of the old cay-dai trees lay like the forms of giant insects seared in a fire, wispy, delicate, dead. It was rumored during those days that the Palace was being held by a unit of student volunteers who had taken the invasion of Hue as a sign and had rushed to join the North Vietnamese. (Another rumor of those days, the one about some 5,000 "shallow graves" outside the city, containing the bodies from NVA executions, had just now been shown to be true.)

But once the walls had been taken and the grounds entered, there was no one left inside except for the dead. They bobbed in the moat and littered all the approaches. The Marines moved in then, and empty ration cans and muddied sheets from the *Stars and Stripes* were added to the litter. A fat Marine had been photographed pissing into the locked-open mouth of a decomposing North Vietnamese soldier.

"No good," Major Trong said. "'No good. Fight here very hard, very bad."

I'd been talking to Sergeant Dang about the Palace and about the line of emperors. When we stalled one last time at the foot of a moat bridge, I'd been asking him the name of the last emperor to occupy the throne. He smiled and shrugged, not so much as if he didn't know, more like it didn't matter.

"Major Trong is emperor now," he said, and gunned the jeep into the Palace grounds.

Khe Sanh

I

During the bad maximum incoming days of the late winter of 1968 there was a young Marine at Khe Sanh whose Vietnam tour had run out. Nearly five of his thirteen months in-country had been spent there at the Khe Sanh Combat Base with the 26th Marines, who had been slowly building to full and then reinforced regimental strength since the previous spring. He could remember a time, not long before, when the 26th considered themselves lucky to be there, when the guys talked of it as though it were a reward for whatever their particular outfits had been through. As far as this Marine was concerned, the reward was for an ambush that fall on the Cam Lo–Con Thien road, when his unit had taken 40 percent casualties, when he himself had taken shrapnel in the chest and arms. (Oh, he'd tell you, but he had seen some shit in this war.) That was when Con Thien was the name everyone knew, long before Khe Sanh had taken on the proportions of a siege camp and lodged itself as an obsession in the heart of the Command, long before a single round had ever fallen inside the perimeter to take off his friends and make his sleep something indistinguishable from waking. He remembered when there was time to play in the streams below the plateau of the base, when all anybody ever talked about were the six shades of green that touched the surrounding hills, when he

the meanest motherfucker in the Valley, but he had tried later, without much success, to scrub it off because, he explained, every damn dude in the DMZ had that written on their flak jackets. And he'd smile.

He was smiling on this last morning of his tour. His gear was straight, his papers in order, his duffel packed, and he was going through all of the last-minute business of going home, the back-slapping and goosing; the joshing with the Old Man ("Come on, you know you're gonna miss this place." "Yes sir. Oh wow!"); the exchanging of addresses; the odd, fragmented reminiscences blurted out of awkward silences. He had a few joints left, wrapped up in a plastic bag (he hadn't smoked them, because, like most Marines at Khe Sanh, he'd expected a ground attack, and he didn't want to be stoned when it came), and he gave these to his best friend, or, rather, his best surviving friend. His oldest friend had been blown away in January, on the same day that the ammo dump had been hit. He had always wondered whether Gunny, the company gunnery sergeant, had known about all the smoking. After three wars Gunny probably didn't care much; besides, they all knew that Gunny was into some pretty cool shit himself. When he dropped by the bunker they said goodbye, and then there wasn't anything to do with the morning but to run in and out of the bunker for a look at the sky, coming back in every time to say that it really ought to clear enough by ten for the planes to get in. By noon, when the goodbyes and take-cares and get-a-little-for-me's had gone on for too long by hours, the sun started to show through the mist. He picked up his duffel and a small AWOL bag and started for the airstrip and the small, deep slit trench on the edge of the strip.

and over in their heads, waiting for the cargo hatch to drop, ten to fifty Marines and correspondents huddled down in the trench, worked their lips futilely to ease the dryness, and then, at the exact same instant, they would all race, collide, stampede, exchanging places. If the barrage was a particularly heavy one, the faces would all distort in the most simple kind of panic, the eyes going wider than the eyes of horses caught in a fire. What you saw was a translucent blur, sensible only at the immediate center, like a swirly-chic photograph of Carnival, and you'd glimpse a face, a shell fragment cased in white sparks, a piece of gear somehow suspended in air, a drift of smoke, and you'd move around the flight crews working the heavy cargo strapping, over scout dogs, over the casually arranged body bags that always lay not far from the strip, covered with flies. And men would still be struggling on or off as the aircraft turned slowly to begin the taxi before the most accelerated take-off the machine had it in it to make. If you were on board, that first movement was an ecstasy. You'd all sit there with empty, exhausted grins, covered with the impossible red dust that laterite breaks down to, dust like scales, feeling the delicious afterchill of the fear, that one quick convulsion of safety. There was no feeling in the world as good as being airborne out of Khe Sanh.

On this last morning, the young Marine caught a ride from his company position that dropped him off fifty meters from the strip. As he moved on foot he heard the distant sound of the C-123 coming in, and that was all he heard. There was hardly more than a hundred-foot ceiling, scary, bearing down on him. Except for the approaching engines, everything was still. If there had been something more, just one incoming round, he might have been all

every bad sign. If he has the imagnation, or the experience of war, he will precognize his own death a thousand times a day, but he will always have enough left to do the one big thing, to Get Out.

Something more was working on the young Marine, and Gunny knew what it was. In this war they called it "acute environmental reaction," but Vietnam has spawned a jargon of such delicate locutions that it's often impossible to know even remotely the thing being described. Most Americans would rather be told that their son is undergoing acute environmental reaction than to hear that he is suffering from shell shock, because they could no more cope with the fact of shell shock than they could with the reality of what had happened to this boy during his five months at Khe Sanh.

Say that his legs just weren't working. It was clearly a medical matter, and the sergeant was going to have to see that something was done about it. But when I left, the kid was still there, sitting relaxed on his duffel and smiling, saying, "Man, when I get home, I'll have it knocked."

II

The terrain above II Corps, where it ran along the Laotian border and into the DMZ, was seldom referred to as the Highlands by Americans. It had been a matter of military expediency to impose a new set of references over Vietnam's older, truer being, an imposition that began most simply with the division of one country into two and continued —it had its logic—with the further division of South Vietnam into four clearly defined tactical corps. It had been one of the exigencies of the war, and if it effectively obliterated even some of the most

many Americans suffered their part of the war there.

Because the Highlands of Vietnam are spooky, unbearably spooky, spooky beyond belief. They are a run of erratic mountain ranges, gnarled valleys, jungled ravines and abrupt plains where Montagnard villages cluster, thin and disappear as the terrain steepens. The Montagnards in all of their tribal components make up the most primitive and mysterious portion of the Vietnamese population, a population that has always confused Americans even in its most Westernized segments. Strictly speaking, the Montagnards are not really Vietnamese at all, certainly not *South* Vietnamese, but a kind of upgraded, demi-enlightened Annamese aborigine, often living in nakedness and brooding silence in their villages. Most Vietnamese and most Montagnards consider each other inferior, and while many Montagnards hired out as mercenaries to the American Special Forces, that older, racially based enmity often slowed down the Allied effort. Many Americans considered them to be nomadic, but the war had had more to do with that than anything in their temperament. We napalmed off their crops and flattened their villages, and then admired the restlessness in their spirit. Their nakedness, their painted bodies, their recalcitrance, their silent composure before strangers, their benign savagery and the sheer, awesome ugliness of them combined to make most Americans who were forced to associate with them a little uncomfortable over the long run. It would seem fitting, ordained, that they should live in the Highlands, among triple canopies, where sudden, contrary mists offered sinister bafflement, where the daily heat and the nighttime cold kept you perpetually, increasingly, on edge, where the silences were interrupted only by

ments and interests aside, simply because we thought it would be easy. But after the Ia Drang, that first arrogance sat less and less well about the shoulders of the Command; it never vanished. There was never again a real guerrilla war after Ia Drang, except in the Delta, and the old Giap stratagem of interdicting the South through the Highlands, cutting the country in two, came to be taken seriously, even obsessively, by many influential Americans.

Oh, that terrain! The bloody, maddening uncanniness of it! When the hideous Battle of Dak To ended at the top of Hill 875, we announced that 4,000 of them had been killed; it had been the purest slaughter, our losses were bad, but clearly it was another American victory. But when the top of the hill was reached, the number of NVA found was four. Four. Of course more died, hundreds more, but the corpses kicked and counted and photographed and buried numbered four. Where, Colonel? And how, and why? Spooky. Everything up there was spooky, and it would have been that way even if there had been no war. You were there in a place where you didn't belong, where things were glimpsed for which you would have to pay and where things went unglimpsed for which you would also have to pay, a place where they didn't play with the mystery but killed you straight off for trespassing. The towns had names that laid a quick, chilly touch on your bones: Kontum, Dak Mat Lop, Dak Roman Peng, Poli Klang, Buon Blech, Pleiku, Pleime, Plei Vi Drin. Just moving through those towns or being based somewhere above them spaced you out, and every time I'd have that vision of myself lying dead somewhere, it was always up there, in the Highlands. It was enough to make an American commander sink to his knees and plead, "O God! Just *once*, let it be our way.

cover, ridge after ridge, murderous slides and gorges, all cloaked by triple canopy and thick monsoon mists. And whole divisions were out there in that.

Marine Intelligence (While I see many hoofmarks going in, I see none coming out), backed by the findings of increasing Air Force reconnaissance missions, had been watching and evaluating the build-up with alarm since spring. Khe Sanh had always been in the vicinity of major infiltration routes, "sat astride" them, as the Mission put it. That slight but definite plateau, rising abruptly from the foothills bridging Laos and Vietnam, had been of value for as long as the Vietnamese had been at war. The routes now used by the NVA had been used twenty years earlier by the Viet Minh. Khe Sanh's original value to the Americans might be gauged by the fact that in spite of the known infiltration all around it, we held it for years with nothing more than a Special Forces A Team; less than a dozen Americans and around 400 indigenous troops, Vietnamese and Montagnard. When the Special Forces first moved in there in 1962, they built their teamhouse, outbuildings, club and defenses over bunkers that had been left by the French. Infiltrating columns simply diverted their routes a kilometer or so away from the central Khe Sanh position. The Green Berets ran out regular, extremely cautious patrols. Since they were almost always surrounded by the infiltrators, Khe Sanh was not the most comfortable duty in Vietnam, but there was seldom anything more than the random ambush or the occasional mortaring that was standard for A Teams anywhere in-country. If the NVA had considered Khe Sanh tactically crucial or even important, they could have taken it at any time. And if we had thought of it as anything more than

rines were airlifted into what was now being called the Khe Sanh Combat Base. The Seabees laid down a 600-meter tarmac airstrip. A beer hall and an air-conditioned officers' club were built, and the regimental command set up its Tactical Operations Center in the largest of the deserted French bunkers. Yet Khe Sanh continued to be only a moderate, private concern of the Marine Corps. A few old hands in the press corps knew vaguely about the base and about the small ville of about a thousand Montagnards which lay four kilometers to the south. It was not until November, when the regiment had grown to full and then reinforced strength (6,000 Marines, not including units added from the 9th Marine Regiment), with 600 Vietnamese Rangers, two detachments of Seabees, a helicopter squadron and a small Special Forces Compound, that the Marines began "leaking" the rather remarkable claim that by building up the base we had lured an unbelievable number of enemy to the area.

It was at about this time that copies of the little red British paperback edition of Jules Roy's *The Battle of Dienbienphu* began appearing wherever members of the Vietnam press corps gathered. You'd spot them around the terrace bar of the Continental Hotel, in L'Amiral Restaurant and Aterbea, at the 8th Aerial Port of Tan Son Nhut, in the Marine-operated Danang Press Center and in the big briefing room of JUSPAO in Saigon, where every afternoon at 4:45 spokesmen conducted the daily war briefing which was colloquially referred to as the Five O'Clock Follies, an Orwellian grope through the day's events as seen by the Mission. (It was very hard-line.) Those who could find copies were reading Bernard Fall's Dien

what we were doing at Khe Sanh in the first place, the repeated evocations of Dien Bien Phu were unnerving. But then, on what briefers liked to call "our side of the ledger," there were important differences.

The base at Khe Sanh was raised, if only slightly, on a plateau which would have slowed a ground attack and given the Marines a gentle vantage from which to fire. The Marines also had a massive reaction force to count on, or at least to hope for. For publication, this consisted of the 1st Air Cavalry Division and elements of the 101st Airborne, but in fact the force numbered almost a quarter of a million men, men at support firebases across the DMZ, planners in Saigon (and Washington) and, most important of all, pilots and crews from headquarters as far away as Udorn, Guam, and Okinawa, men whose energies and attentions became fixed almost exclusively on Khe Sanh missions. Air support was everything, the cornerstone of all our hopes at Khe Sanh, and we knew that once the monsoons lifted, it would be nothing to drop tens of thousands of tons of high explosives and napalm all around the base, to supply it without strain, to cover and reinforce the Marines.

It was a comfort, all of that power and precision and exquisitely geared clout. It meant a lot to the thousands of Marines at Khe Sanh, to the Command, to correspondents spending a few days and nights at the base, to officials in the Pentagon. We could all sleep easier for it: lance corporals and General Westmoreland, me and the President, Navy medics and the parents of all the boys inside the wire. All any of us had to worry about was the fact that Khe Sanh was vastly outnumbered and entirely surrounded; that, and the knowledge that all ground evacuation routes, including the vital

plenty of stories about entire squads wiped out (their mutilated bodies would so enrage Marines that they would run out "vengeance patrols" which often enough ended the same way), companies taking 75 percent casualties, Marines ambushing Marines, artillery and airstrikes called in on our own positions, all in the course of routine Search-and-Destroy operations. And you knew that, sooner or later, if you went with them often enough, it would happen to you too.

And the grunts themselves knew: the madness, the bitterness, the horror and doom of it. They were hip to it, and more: they savored it. It was no more insane than most of what was going down, and often enough it had its refracted logic. "Eat the apple, fuck the Corps," they'd say, and write it up on their helmets and flak jackets for their officers to see. (One kid tattooed it on his shoulder.) And sometimes they'd look at you and laugh silently and long, the laugh on them and on you for being with them when you didn't have to be. And what could be funnier, really, given all that an eighteen-year-old boy could learn in a month of patrolling the Z? It was that joke at the deepest part of the blackest kernel of fear, and you could die laughing. They even wrote a song, a letter to the mother of a dead Marine, that went something like, "Tough shit, tough shit, you kid got greased, but what the fuck, he was just a grunt. . . ." They got savaged a lot and softened a lot, their secret brutalized them and darkened them and very often it made them beautiful. It took no age, seasoning or education to make them know exactly where true violence resided.

And they were killers. Of course they were; what would anyone expect them to be? It absorbed them, inhabited them, made them strong in the way that

had committed themselves on such a scale that engagement was inevitable. No one I knew doubted that it would come, probably in the form of a massive ground attack, and that when it came it would be terrible and great.

Tactically, its value to the Command was thought so great that General Westmoreland could announce that the Tet Offensive was merely Phase II of a brilliant Giap strategy. Phase I had been revealed in the autumn skirmishes between Loc Ninh and Dak To. Phase III ("the capstone," the general called it) was to be Khe Sanh. It seems impossible that anyone, at any time, even in the chaos of Tet, could have actually called something as monumental (and decisive?) as that offensive a mere diversion for something as negligible as Khe Sanh, but all of that is on record.

And by then, Khe Sanh was famous, one of the very few place names in Vietnam that was recognized by the American public. Khe Sanh said "siege," it said "encircled Marines" and "heroic defenders." It could be understood by newspaper readers quickly, it breathed Glory and War and Honored Dead. It seemed to make sense. It was good stuff. One can only imagine the anxiety which the Commander in Chief suffered over it. Lyndon Johnson said it straight out, he did not want "any damn Dinbinfoo," and he did something unprecedented in the history of warfare. The Joint Chiefs of Staff were summoned and made to sign a statement "for the public reassurance," asserting that Khe Sanh could and would be held at all costs. (Apparently, *Coriolanus* had never been required reading at the Point. Noncoms in the field, even grunts with no career ambitions, felt the professional indignity of the President's gambit, talked of it as something shameful.) Perhaps Khe Sanh would

everywhere you could smell that sour reek of obsolescence that followed the Marines all over Vietnam. If they could not hear their own dead from Con Thien, only three months past, how could they ever be expected to hear the dead from Dien Bien Phu?

Not a single round had fallen inside the perimeter. The jungled slopes running up from the bowl of the base were not yet burned over and hung with the flare chutes that looked like infants' shrouds. Six shades of green, motherfucker, tell me that ain't something beautiful. There were no heaps of shredded, blood-soaked jungle fatigues outside the triage room, and the wires were not cluttered each dawn with their dead. None of it had happened yet when Khe Sanh became lost forever as a tactical entity. It is impossible to fix the exact moment in time when it happened, or to know, really, why. All that was certain was that Khe Sanh had become a passion, the false love object in the heart of the Command. It cannot even be determined which way the passion traveled. Did it proceed from the filthiest ground-zero slit trench and proceed outward, across I Corps to Saigon and on (taking the true perimeter with it) to the most abstract reaches of the Pentagon? Or did it get born in those same Pentagon rooms where six years of failure had made the air bad, where optimism no longer sprang from anything viable but sprang and sprang, all the way to Saigon, where it was packaged and shipped north to give the grunts some kind of reason for what was about to happen to them? In its outlines, the promise was delicious: Victory! A vision of as many as 40,000 of them out there in the open, fighting it out on our terms, fighting for once like men, fighting to no avail. There would

laughing a bad laugh and then going more silent than even deep sleep permits before starting it up again, and it is more terrible in there than any place I can even imagine. I got up then and went outside, any place at all was better than this, and stood in the dark smoking a cigarette, watching the hills for a sign and hoping none would come because, shit, what could be revealed except more fear? Three in the morning, and my blood is intimate with the chill, host to it, and very willing too. From the center of the earth there is a tremor that shakes everything, running up through my legs and body, shaking my head, yet no one in the bunker wakes up. We called them "'Archlights," he called them Rolling Thunder, and it was incessant during the nights. The bombs would release at 18,000 feet and the planes would turn and fly back to Udorn or Guam. Dawn seems to last until late morning, dusk falls at four. Everything I see is blown through with smoke, everything is on fire everywhere. It doesn't matter that memory distorts; every image, every sound comes back out of smoke and the smell of things burning.

Some of it, like smoke from an exploding round in the air, breaks cleanly and at a comfortable distance. Some of it pours out of large tubs of shit being burned off with diesel fuel, and it hangs, hangs, taking you full in the throat even though you are used to it. Right there on the strip a fuel ship has been hit, and no one who has heard that can kill the shakes for an hour. (What woke you? . . . What woke you?) A picture comes in, absolutely still for a moment, and then resumes the motion it once had: a heat tablet, burning in high intensity, covered by a tiny, blackened stove a Marine had made for me two weeks before in Hue out of the small dessert can from a ration box. From

the mists return. Then it is night again, and the sky beyond the western perimeter is burning with slowly dropping magnesium flares. Heaps of equipment are on fire, terrifying in their jagged black massiveness, burning prehistoric shapes like the tail of a C-130 sticking straight up in the air, dead metal showing through the gray-black smoke. God, if it can do that to metal, what will it do to me? And then something very near me is smoldering, just above my head, the damp canvas coverings on the sandbags lining the top of a slit trench. It is a small trench, and a lot of us have gotten into it in a hurry. At the end farthest from me there is a young guy who has been hit in the throat, and he is making the sounds a baby will make when he is trying to work up the breath for a good scream. We were on the ground when those rounds came, and a Marine nearer the trench had been splattered badly across the legs and groin. I sort of took him into the trench with me. It was so crowded I couldn't help leaning on him a little, and he kept saying, "You motherfucker, you cocksucker," until someone told him that I wasn't a grunt but a reporter. Then he started to say, very quietly, "Be careful, Mister. Please be careful." He'd been wounded before, and he knew how it would hurt in a few minutes. People would just get ripped up in the worst ways there, and things were always on fire. Far up the road that skirted the TOC was a dump where they burned the gear and uniforms that nobody needed anymore. On top of the pile I saw a flak jacket so torn apart that no one would ever want it again. On the back, its owner had listed the months that he had served in Vietnam. *March, April, May* (each month written out in a tentative, spidery hand), *June, July, August, September, Octobler, Novembler, Decembler, Jan-*

sleep. No one who heard it was able to smile that bitter, secret survivor's smile that was the reflex to almost all news of disaster. It was too awful even for that.

Five kilometers southwest of the Khe Sanh Combat Base, sitting above the river which forms the border with Laos, there was a Special Forces A Camp. It was called Langvei, taking its name from the small Montagnard village nearby which had been mistakenly bombed a year before by the Air Force. The camp was larger than most Special Forces camps, and much better built. It was set on twin hills about 700 meters apart, and the vital bunkers holding most of the troops were on the hill nearest the river. It was manned by twenty-four Americans and over 400 Vietnamese troops. Its bunkers were deep, solid, with three feet of reinforced concrete overhead, seemingly impregnable. And sometime after midnight, the North Vietnamese came and took it. They took it with a style that had been seen only once before, in the Ia Drang, attacking with weapons and tactics which no one imagined they had. Nine light tanks, Soviet T-34's and 76's, were deployed east and west, closing on the camp so suddenly that the first sound of them was mistaken by the Americans for a malfunction of the camp generator. Satchel charges, bangalore torpedoes, tear gas and—ineffable horror—napalm were all hurled into the machine-gun slits and air vents of the bunkers. It took very little time. An American colonel who had come on an inspection visit to Langvei was seen charging the tanks with nothing but hand grenades before he was cut down. (He survived. The word "miracle" doesn't even apply.) Somewhere between ten and fifteen Americans were killed, and as many as 300 of the indigenous troops. The survivors traveled all night,

world to do with Khe Sanh after Langvei fell. I wanted to ask it so badly that my hesitance made me mad for months. Colonel (I wanted to ask), this is purely hypothetical, I hope you understand. But what if all of those gooks that you think are out there are *really* out there? And what if they attack before the monsoons blow south, some mist-clogged night when our planes just cannot get up there? What if they really want Khe Sanh, want it so badly that they are willing to maneuver over the triple lines of barbed wire, the German razor wire too; over barricades formed by their own dead (a tactic, Colonel, favored by your gook in Korea), coming in waves, *human* waves, and in such numbers that the barrels of our .50-calibers overheat and melt and all the M-16's are jammed, until all of the death in all of the Claymore mines on our defenses has been spent and absorbed? What if they are still coming, moving toward the center of a base so smashed by their artillery that those pissy little trenches and bunkers that *your* Marines half got up are useless, coming as the first MIG's and IL-28's ever seen in this war bomb out the TOC and the strip, the med tent and the control tower (People's Army my ass, right, Colonel?), coming at you 20,000 to 40,000 strong? And what if they pass over every barricade we can put in their way . . . and kill every living thing, defending or retreating . . . and take Khe Sanh?

Some strange things would happen. One morning, at the height of the monsoons, the sun came up brightly at dawn and shone all day. The early-morning skies were a clean, brilliant blue, the only time before April that anyone saw that at Khe Sanh, and instead of waking and coming out shivering from their bunkers, the grunts stripped down

height? He'd been doing the singing, and he was laughing now because he'd made me turn around. His name was Mayhew, it was written out in enormous red letters across the front of his helmet: MAYHEW—*You'd better believe it!* I'd been walking with my flak jacket open, a stupid thing to do even on this morning, and they could see the stitched tag above my left breast pocket with the name of my magazine written on it.

"Correspondent?" the Negro said.

Mayhew just laughed. " 'I'd-a rather be—a Oscar Mayer . . . weenieee,' " he sang. "You can write that, man, tell 'em all I said so."

"Don't pay no attention to him," the Negro said. "That's Mayhew. He's a crazy fucker, ain't you, Mayhew?"

"I sure hope so," Mayhew said. " 'I'd rather be a Oscar Mayer weiner. . . .' "

He was young, nineteen, he later told me, and he was trying to grow a mustache. His only luck with it so far was a few sparse, transparent blond clumps set at odd intervals across his upper lip, and you couldn't see that unless the light was right. The Negro was called Day Tripper. It was on his helmet, along with DETROIT CITY. And on the back, where most guys just listed the months of their tours, he had carefully drawn a full calendar where each day served was marked off with a neat X. They were both from Hotel Company of the 2nd Battalion, which was dug in along the northern perimeter, but they were taking advantage of the day to visit a friend of theirs, a mortar man with 1/26.

"The lieutenant ever hear 'bout this, he know what to do," Day Tripper said.

"Fuck the lieutenant," Mayhew said. "You remember from before he ain't wrapped too tight."

get hungry, it ain't so bad. I'd give my left ball for a can of fruit now."

I always scrounged fruit from rear areas to bring forward, and I had some in my pack. "What kind do you like?" I asked.

"Any kind's good," he said. "Fruit cocktail's really good."

"No, man," Day Tripper said. "Peaches, baby, peaches. All that syrup. Now that's some good shit."

"There you go, Mayhew, I said, tossing him a fruit cocktail. I gave a can of peaches to Day Tripper and kept a can for myself.

We talked while we ate. Mayhew told me about his father, who "got greased in Korea," and about his mother, who worked in a department store in Kansas City. Then he started to tell about Day Tripper, who got his name because he was afraid of the night—not the dark, but the night—and who didn't mind who knew it. There wasn't anything he wouldn't do during daylight, but if there was any way at all to fix it he liked to be deep in his bunker by nightfall. He was always volunteering for the more dangerous daylight patrols, just to make sure he got in by dusk. (This was before daylight patrols, in fact almost all patrols around Khe Sanh, were discontinued.) There were a lot of white guys, especially junior officers trying to be cool, who were always coming on to Day Tripper about his hometown, calling it Dodge City or Motown and laughing. ("Why they think somethin's special about Detroit?" he said. "Ain't nothin' special, ain't nothin' so funny, neither.") He was a big bad spade gone wrong somehow, and no matter how mean he tried to look something constantly gentle showed. He told me he knew guys from Detroit who were taking mortars back, breaking them down so that each

Four more Marines dropped into the pit.

"Where's Evans?" Mayhew demanded. "Any of you guys know Evans?"

One of the mortar men came over.

"Evans is over in Danang," he said. "He caught a little shit the other night."

"That right?" Mayhew said. "Evans get wounded?"

"He hurt bad?" Day Tripper asked.

"Not bad enough," the mortar man said, laughing. "He'll be back in ten days. Just some stuff in the legs."

"He's real lucky," another one said. "Same round got him killed a guy."

"Yeah," someone said. "Greene got killed." He wasn't talking to us, but to the crew, who knew it already. "Remember Greene?" Everyone nodded.

"Wow, Green," he said. "Green was all fixed to get out. He's jerkin' off thirty times a day, that fuckin' guy, and they's all set to give him a medical. And out."

"That's no shit," the other one said. "Thirty times a day. Dis*gus*ting, man. That sombitch had come all over his pants, that fuckin' Greene. He was waitin' outside to see the major about gettin' sent home, an' the major comes out to find him an' he's just sittin' there jerkin' off. Then he gets blown away the night before."

"Well," Day Tripper said quietly to Mayhew, "see what happens if you jerk off?"

A Chinook, forty feet long with rotors front and back, set down on the airstrip by Charlie Med, looking like a great, gross beast getting a body purchase on some mud, blowing bitter gusts of dust, pebbles and debris for a hundred yards around. Everywhere within that circle of wind men turned

Four kilometers northwest of Khe Sanh was Hill 861, the hardest-hit of all the sector outposts after Langvei, and it seemed logical to everyone that the 1st Battalion of the 9th Marine Regiment should have been chosen to defend it. Some even believed that if anyone but 1/9 had been put there, 861 would never have been hit. Of all the hard-luck outfits in Vietnam, this was said to be the most doomed, doomed in its Search-and-Destroy days before Khe Sanh, known for a history of ambush and confusion and for a casualty rate which was the highest of any outfit in the entire war. That was the kind of reputation that takes hold most deeply among the men of the outfit itself, and when you were with them you got a sense of dread that came out of something more terrible than just a collective loss of luck. All the odds seemed somehow sharply reduced, estimates of your own survival were revised horribly downward. One afternoon with 1/9 on 861 was enough to bend your nerves for days, because it took only a few minutes up there to see the very worst of it: the stumbles, the simple motions of a walk suddenly racked by spasms, mouths sand-dry seconds after drinking, the dreamy smiles of total abdication. Hill 861 was the home of the thousand-yard stare, and I prayed hard for a chopper to come and get me away from there, to fly me over the ground fire and land me in the middle of a mortar barrage on the Khe Sanh pad—whatever! Anything was better than this.

On a night shortly after the Langvei attack an entire platoon of 1/9 was ambushed during a patrol and wiped out. Hill 861 had been hit repeatedly, once for three days straight during a perimeter probe that turned into a siege that really *was* a siege. For reasons that no one is certain of, Marine helicopters refused to fly missions up there,

back of his neck, shaking his head from side to side violently, as though in agony. He wasn't wounded.

We were here because I had to pass this way to reach my bunker, where I had to pick up some things to take over to Hotel Company for the night. Day Tripper wasn't liking the route. He looked at the bodies and then at me. It was that look which said, "See? You see what it does?" I had seen that look so many times during the past months that I must have had it too now, and neither of us said anything. Mayhew wasn't letting himself look at anything. It was as though he were walking by himself now, and he was singing in an odd, quiet voice. " 'When you get to San Francisco,' " he sang, " 'be sure and wear some flowers in your hair.' "

We passed the control tower, that target that was its own aiming stake, so prominent and vulnerable that climbing up there was worse than having to run in front of a machine gun. Two of them had already been hit, and the sandbags running up the sides didn't seem to make any difference. We went by the grimy admin buildings and bunkers, a bunch of deserted "hardbacks" with crushed metal roofs, the TOC, the command latrine and a post-office bunker. There was the now roofless beer hall and the collapsed, abandoned officers' club. The Seabee bunker was just a little farther along the road.

It was not like the other bunkers. It was the deepest, safest, cleanest place in Khe Sanh, with six feet of timbers, steel and sandbags overhead, and inside it was brightly lit. The grunts called it the Alamo Hilton and thought it was candy-assed, while almost every correspondent who came to Khe Sanh tried to get a bed there. A bottle of whiskey or a case of beer would be enough to get you in for a few nights, and once you became a friend of the

Mayhew said, laughing. "'Sides, they do it 'cause they know how it fucks you all up."

"Tell me *you* ain' scared shit!"

"You'll never see *me* scared, motherfucker."

"Oh no. Three nights ago you was callin' out for your *momma* while them fuckers was hittin' our wire."

"Boo-sheeit! I ain't gettin' hit in Vietnam."

"Oh no? Okay, mothafucker, why not?"

"'Cause," Mayhew said, "it don't exist." It was an old joke, but this time he wasn't laughing.

By now, the trenchline circled the camp almost completely. Most of the northern perimeter was held down by the 2nd Battalion of the 26th Marine Regiment, and Hotel Company was along this sector. In its westernmost part it was opposed by North Vietnamese trenches that ended just 300 meters away. Farther to the east it sat above a narrow river, and beyond that was Hill 950, three kilometers to the north, which was held by the NVA and whose highest ridge ran exactly parallel to the Khe Sanh airstrip. The bunkers and connecting trenchworks sat on a rise that ran up from the riverbank, and the hills began a couple of hundred meters from the far side of the river. Two hundred meters away, facing the Marine trenches, there was an NVA sniper with a .50-caliber machine gun who shot at the Marines from a tiny spider hole. During the day he fired at anything that rose above the sandbags, and at night he fired at any lights he could see. You could see him clearly from the trench, and if you were looking through the scope of a Marine sniper's rifle you could even see his face. The Marines fired on his position with mortars and recoilless rifles, and he would drop into his hole and wait. Gunships fired rockets at him, and

anything to him, except to yell out, "Come on down, Orrin. You'll get greased for sure, motherfucker." Finally, the gunnery sergeant came along and said, "If you don't get your ass down off that berm I'll shoot you myself."

"Listen," Mayhew said. "Maybe you better go and see the chaplain."

"Real good," Orrin said. "What's that cocksucker gone do for me?"

"Maybe you could get an emergency leave."

"No," someone said. "There's gotta be a death in the family before you'll get out like that."

"Oh, don't worry," Orrin said. "There's gone be a death in my family. Just soon's I git home." And then he laughed.

It was a terrible laugh, very quiet and intense, and it was the thing that made everyone who heard it believe Orrin. After that, he was the crazy fucking grunt who was going to get through the war so he could go home and kill his old lady. It made him someone special in the company. It made a lot of guys think that he was lucky now, that nothing could happen to him, and they stayed as close to him as they could. I even felt some of it, enough to be glad that we would be in the same bunker that night. It made sense. I believed it too, and I would have been really surprised if I had heard later that anything had happened to him. But that was the kind of thing you seldom heard after you left an outfit, the kind of thing you avoided hearing if you could. Maybe he was killed or maybe he changed his mind, but I doubt it. When I remembered Orrin, all I could think of was that there was going to be a shooting in Tennessee.

Once on a two-day pass to Danang, Mayhew had gone off limits and into the black market looking

was the smell of urine, or old, old sweat, C-ration decay, moldy canvas and private crud, and that mixing up of other smells that were special to combat zones. A lot of us believed that exhaustion and fear could be smelled and that certain dreams gave off an odor. (We were regular Hemingway gypsies about some things. No matter how much wind a chopper would put out as it landed, you could always tell when there were body bags around an lz, and the tents where the Lurps lived smelled unlike any other tents anywhere in Vietnam.) This bunker was at least as bad as any I'd ever been in, and I gagged in there once, the first time. Because there was almost no light, you had to imagine most of what you smelled, and that became something like a pastime. I hadn't realized how black Day Tripper was until we walked inside the bunker.

"It *def*initely stinks somethin' fierce in here," he said. "I gotta be gettin' a mo'—uh—ef*fec*tive deodorant."

He paused.

"Any kinda shit come up tonight, you jus' keep with me. You be lucky Mayhew don't think you a Zip an' blast your fuckin' head off. He'll go pretty crazy sometimes."

"You think we'll be hit?"

He shrugged. "He might try an' do a probe. He did that number 'gainst us three nights ago an' kill one boy. Kill a Brother.

"But this here's a real good bunker. We took some shit right on top here. All kindsa dirt come down on top our heads, but we'se all right."

"Are guys sleeping in their flak jackets?"

"Some do. I don'. Mayhew, crazy fucker, he sleep bare-ass. He so tough, man, li'l fucker, the hawk is out, an' he's in here bare-ass."

"What's that? About the hawk?"

say to you, ever. Not one word. An' I *know* . . . oh man, I jus' *know* you already signed that paper."

Mayhew didn't say anything. It was hard to believe that the two were around the same age.

"What I gonna do with you, poor fucker? Why . . . why you jus' don' go runnin' out th' wire there? Let 'em gun you down an' get it over with. Here, man, here's a grenade. Why you jus' don' go up backa the shithouse an' pull the pin an' lie down on it?"

"You're fuckin' unbe*liev*able. Man, it's just four months!"

"Four months? Baby, four *seconds* in this whorehouse'll get you greased. An' after your poppa an' all that. An' you jus' ain' *learned*. You're the sorriest sorriest grunt mother I ever seen. No, man, but the *sorriest!* Fuckin' Mayhew, man. I feel sorry for you."

"Day Tripper? Hey, it'll be okay. Y'know?"

"Sure, baby. Jus' don't talk to me right away. Clean your rifle. Write your momma. Do *somethin'*. Talk to me later."

"We can smoke some bullshit."

"Okay, baby. Say later." He walked back into the bunker and lay down. Mayhew took off his hemlet and scratched out something written on the side. It had read *20 April and* OUTTA SIGHT!

Sometimes you'd step from the bunker, all sense of time passing having left you, and find it dark out. The far side of the hills around the bowl of the base glimmering, but you could never see the source of the light, and it had the look of a city at night approached from a great distance. Flares were dropping everywhere around the fringes of the perimeter, laying a dead white light on the high ground rising from the piedmont. There would be

one, that you were safe, or at least saved. If you were still standing up and looking after that, you deserved anything that happened to you.

Nights were when the air and artillery strikes were heaviest, because that was when we knew that the NVA was above ground and moving. At night you could lie out on some sandbags and watch the C-47's mounted with Vulcans doing their work. The C-47 was a standard prop flareship, but many of them carried .20- and .762-mm. guns on their doors, Mike-Mikes that could fire out 300 rounds per second, Gatling style, "a round in every square inch of a football field in less than a minute," as the handouts said. They used to call it Puff the Magic Dragon, but the Marines knew better: they named it Spooky. Every fifth round fired was a tracer, and when Spooky was working, everything stopped while that solid stream of violent red poured down out of the black sky. If you watched from a great distance, the stream would seem to dry up between bursts, vanishing slowly from air to ground like a comet tail, the sound of the guns disappearing too, a few seconds later. If you watched at a close range, you couldn't believe that anyone would have the courage to deal with that night after night, week after week, and you cultivated a respect for the Viet Cong and the NVA who had crouched under it every night now for months. It was awesome, worse than anything the Lord had ever put down on Egypt, and at night, you'd hear the Marines talking, watching it, yelling, "Get some!" until they grew quiet and someone would say, "Spooky understands." The nights were very beautiful. Night was when you really had the least to fear and feared the most. You could go through some very bad numbers at night.

Because, really, what a choice there was; what

though you could kick it all away and come back. You could fall down dead so that the medics would have to spend half an hour looking for the hole that killed you, getting more and more spooked as the search went on. You could be shot, mined, grenaded, rocketed, mortared, sniped at, blown up and away so that your leavings had to be dropped into a sagging poncho and carried to Graves Registration, that's all she wrote. It was almost marvelous.

And at night, all of it seemed more possible. At night in Khe Sanh, waiting there, thinking about all of them (40,000, some said), thinking that they might really try it, could keep you up. If they did, when they did, it might not matter that you were in the best bunker in the DMZ, wouldn't matter that you were young and had plans, that you were loved, that you were a noncombatant, an observer. Because if it came, it would be in a bloodswarm of killing, and credentials would not be examined. (The only Vietnamese many of us knew was the words "Bao Chi! Bao Chi!"—Journalist! Journalist! or even "Bao Chi Fap!"—French journalist!, which was the same as crying, Don't shoot! Don't shoot!) You came to love your life, to love and respect the mere fact of it, but often you became heedless of it in the way that somnambulists are heedless. Being "good" meant staying alive, and sometimes that was only a matter of caring enough at any given moment. No wonder everyone became a luck freak, no wonder you could wake at four in the morning some mornings and *know* that tomorrow it would finally happen, you could stop worrying about it now and just lie there, sweating in the dampest chill you ever felt.

But once it was actually going on, things were different. You were just like everyone else, you

"Hey Mayhew, turn that fuckin' thing off."

"Right after Sports," Mayhew said. He was naked now, sitting up in his bed and hunched over the radio as though the light and the voice were a miracle for him. He was cleaning his face with some Wash 'n Dri's.

"It's been proven!" someone said. "You take and put a Chevvy in a Ford and a Ford in a Chevvy and they *both* go faster. It's been proven!"

We were all ready for sleep. Mayhew was the only one with his boots off. Two Marines that I hadn't even met before nightfall had gone out on the scrounge and came back with a new stretcher for me to sleep on, giving it to me without looking at me, as if to say, *Shit*, it ain't anything, we *like* walking around above ground. They were always doing things like that for you, the way Mayhew had tried to give me his mattress, the way grunts in Hue one day had tried to give me their helmets and flak jackets because I had turned up without my own. If you tore your fatigues on the wire or trying to crawl for cover, you'd have new or at least fresh ones within minutes and never know where they came from. They always took care of you.

". . . so next time," the announcer said, "*think* about it. It *might* just save your life." Another voice came on: "All right, then, moving right along here with our fabulous Sounds of the Sixties, AFVN, Armed Forces Radio Network, Vietnam, and for all you guys in the First of the Forty-fourth, and especially for the Soul Brother in the Orderly Room, here's Otis Redding—the *immortal* Otis Redding, singing 'Dock of the Bay.' "

"All right, my man," Day Tripper said.

"Listen," one of the Marines said. "When you think of all the guys in this fucked-up war, them

"Hey, cocksuck, you just tol' me to turn it off."

"Come on, man, that's an outtasight song."

Mayhew turned it up. It still wasn't very loud, but it filled the bunker. It was a song that had been on the radio a lot that winter.

There's something happening here,
What it is ain't exactly clear.
There's a man with a gun over there,
Tellin' me I've got to beware.
I think it's time we stopped, children,
What's that sound?
Everybody look what's goin' down. . . .

"Know what I heard over at the captain's hootch?" Mayhew said. "Some kid tol' me the Cav's comin' in here."

"Right," someone said. "They're coming tomorrow."

"What *time* tomorrow?"

"All right," Mayhew said. "Don't believe me. This kid was a clerk. He's over to the TOC yesterday and he heard 'em talking."

"What's the Cav gonna do here? Make this a fuckin' parking lot for helicopters?"

The Marines did not like the Cav, the 1st Cavalry Division (Airmobile), they liked them even less than they liked the rest of the Army, and at the same time members of the Cav were beginning to feel as though their sole mission in Vietnam was to bail out Marines in trouble. They had come to help the Marines a dozen times in the past six months, and the last time, during the battle of Hue, they had taken almost as many casualties as the Marines had. There had been rumors about a relief operation for Khe Sanh since February, and by now they were being taken about as seriously as

the dark without any memory of their having been lighted.

"Probe," Mayhew said. He was leaning over me, completely dressed again, his face almost touching mine, and for a second I had the idea that he might have run over to cover me from any possible incoming. (It would not have been the first time that a grunt had done that.) Everyone was awake, all of our poncho liners were thrown back, I reached for my glasses and helmet and realized that I'd already put them on. Day Tripper was looking at us. Mayhew was grinning.

"Listen to that fucker, listen to that, that fucker's gonna burn out the barrel for sure."

It was an M-60 machine gun and it was not firing in bursts, but in a mad, sustained manner. The gunner must have seen something; maybe he was firing cover for a Marine patrol trying to get back in through the wire, maybe it was a three- or four-man probe that had been caught in the flare-light, something standing or moving, an infiltrator or a rat, but it sounded like the gunner was holding off a division. I couldn't tell whether there was answering fire or not, and then, abruptly, the firing stopped.

"Let's go see," Mayhew said, grabbing his rifle.

"Don't you go messin' with that out there," Day Tripper said. "They need us, they be sendin' for us. Fuckin' Mayhew."

"Man, it's all over. Listen. Come on," he said to me. "See if we can get you a story."

"Give me a second." I put on my flak jacket and we left the bunker, Day Tripper shaking his head at us, saying, "Fuckin' Mayhew. . . ."

Before, the fire had sounded as though it were coming from directly above the bunker, but the Marines on watch there said it had been from a

There was a dull pop in the air above us, and an illumination round fell drowsily over the wire.

"Slope," Mayhew said. "See him there, see there, on the wire there?"

I couldn't see anything out there, there was no movement, and the screaming had stopped. As the flare dimmed, the sobbing started up and built quickly until it was a scream again.

A Marine brushed past us. He had a mustache and a piece of camouflaged parachute silk fastened bandana-style around his throat, and on his hip he wore a holster which held an M-79 grenade-launcher. For a second I thought I'd hallucinated him. I hadn't heard him approaching, and I tried now to see where he might have come from, but I couldn't. The M-79 had been cut down and fitted with a special stock. It was obviously a well-loved object; you could see the kind of work that had gone into it by the amount of light caught from the flares that glistened on the stock. The Marine looked serious, dead-eyed serious, and his right hand hung above the holster, waiting. The screaming had stopped again.

"Wait," he said. "I'll fix that fucker."

His hand was resting now on the handle of the weapon. The sobbing began again, and the screaming; we had the pattern now, the North Vietnamese was screaming the same thing over and over, and we didn't need a translator to tell us what it was.

"Put that fucker away," the Marine said, as though to himself. He drew the weapon, opened the breach and dropped in a round that looked like a great swollen bullet, listening very carefully all the while to the shrieking. He placed the M-79 over his left forearm and aimed for a second before firing. There was an enormous flash on the wire 200 meters away, a spray of orange sparks, and

your buttocks. You don't have to be a seasoned tactician to realize that your ass is cold.

Interviews with the commander of the 26th Marine Regiment, Colonel David Lownds, seemed to reveal a man who was utterly insensible to the gravity of his position, but Lownds was a deceptively complicated man with a gift (as one of his staff officers put it) for "jerking off the press." He could appear as a meek, low-keyed, distracted and even stupid man (some reporters referred to him privately as "The Lion of Khe Sanh"), as though he had been carefully picked for just these qualities by a cynical Command as a front for its decisions. When confronted with the possible odds against a successful defense of Khe Sanh, he would say things like "I do not plan on reinforcements" or "I'm not worried. I've got Marines." He was a small man with vague, watery eyes, slightly reminiscent of a rodent in a fable, with one striking feature; a full, scrupulously attended regimental mustache.

His professed ignorance of Dien Bien Phu drove correspondents crazy, but it was a dodge. Lownds knew very well about Dien Bien Phu and what had happened there, knew more about it than most of the interviewers. When I first met him, I brought a two-week-old message to Khe Sanh from his son-in-law, a Marine captain whom I'd met in Hue. He had been badly wounded in the fighting along the canals southwest of the Citadel, and the message amounted to little more than personal regards. Being a colonel commanding a regiment, Lownds of course had all the current information on the captain's condition, but he seemed glad for the chance to talk to someone who'd been there, who had seen him. He was proud of his son-in-law and very touched by the remembrance. He was also growing tired of reporters and of the criticism

widjis." He had tough, shrewd eyes that matched his voice and a disdain for Command bravado that could be unsettling in an interview.

We flew the DMZ together from Quang Tri to Camp Carrol and the Rockpile, hitting each of the firebases that had been set up or converted to firing missions supporting Khe Sanh. We flew in beat-up Marine choppers, clumsy H-34's (Screw metal fatigue, we decided; the 34 had a lot of heart), over the cold, shattered, mist-bound hills, the same hills that had received over 120,000,000 pounds of explosives from B-52 raids in the previous three weeks, terrain like moonscapes, crated and pitted and full of skilled North Vietnamese gunners. From past experience and the estimates of our meteorologists, the monsoons should be ending now, blowing south, clearing the DMZ skies and leaving the hills warm, but it wasn't happening, the monsoon held ("The weather?" some colonel would say. "The weather is increasingly advantageous!"), we were freezing, you could barely piss on those hilltop firebases, and the ceilings were uniformly low before noon and after three. On the last part of the trip, flying into Dong Ha, the aluminum rod that held the seats broke, spilling us to the floor and making the exact sound that a .50-caliber round will make when it strikes a chopper, giving us all a bad scare and then a good, good laugh. A couple of times the pilots thought they saw something moving on the hilltops and we went down, circling five or six times while we all groaned and giggled from fear and the cold. The crew chief was a young Marine who moved around the chopper without a safety line hooked to his flight suit, so comfortable with the rolling and shaking of the ship that you couldn't even pause to admire his daredevil nerve; you cut straight through to his easy

covered over, obscured from the eyes of unauthorized personnel.

We sat down, the general offered us cigarettes (by the pack) and Prager began the questioning. It was all stuff I'd heard before, a synthesis of everything Prager had gotten together during the past four days. I'd never seen any point in asking generals heavy questions about anything; they were officials too, and the answers were almost always what you expected them to be. I half listened, tuning in and out, and Prager began a long, involved question dealing with weather variants, air capability, elevation and range of our big guns, his big guns, problems of supply and reinforcement and (apologetically) disengagement and evacuation. The general touched his fingertips together as the question developed, smiled and nodded as it went into its third minute, he looked impressed by Prager's grasp of the situation and, finally, when the question ended, he placed his hands on the desk. He was still smiling.

"What?" he said.

Prager and I looked at each other quickly.

"You'll have to excuse me, boys. I'm a little hard of hearing. I don't always catch it all."

So Prager did it again, speaking unnaturally loud, and my mind went back to the map, into it really, so that the sound of outgoing artillery beyond the general's windows and the smell of burning shit and wet canvas brought in on the cold air put my head back at Khe Sanh for a moment.

I thought about the grunts who had sat in a circle one night with a guitar, singing "Where Have All the Flowers Gone?" Jack Laurence of CBS News had asked them if they knew what that song meant to so many people, and they said, Yes, yes, they knew. I thought about the graffiti that John Wheeler

Marine Headquarters, was coming over to brief us on developments in the DMZ and Khe Sanh. The colonel in charge of "press operations" was visibly nervous, the dining room was being cleared for the meeting, microphones set up, chairs arranged, printed material put in order. These official briefings usually did the same thing to your perception of the war that flares did to your night vision, but this one was supposed to be special, and correspondents had come in from all over I Corps to be there. Among us was Peter Braestrup of the *Washington Post,* formerly of *The New York Times.* He had been covering the war for nearly three years. He had been a captain in the Marines in Korea; ex-Marines are like ex-Catholics or off-duty Feds, and Braestrup still made the Marines a special concern of his. He had grown increasingly bitter about the Marines' failure to dig in at Khe Sanh, about their shocking lack of defenses against artillery. He sat quietly as the colonel introduced the general and the briefing began.

The weather was excellent: "The sun is up over Khe Sanh by ten every morning." (A collective groan running through the seated journalists.) "I'm glad to be able to tell you that Route Nine is now open and completely accessible." (Would you drive Route 9 into Khe Sanh, General? You bet you wouldn't.)

"What about the Marines at Khe Sanh?" someone asked.

"I'm glad we've come to that," the general said. "I was at Khe Sanh for several hours this morning, and I want to tell you that those Marines there are *clean!*"

There was a weird silence. We all knew we'd heard him, the man had said that the Marines at Khe Sanh were clean ("Clean? He said 'clean,'

VI

The door gunner was leaning out, looking down, and he started to laugh. He wrote out a note and handed it to me. It read, "We sure brang some pee down to bear on them hills."

The monsoons were breaking, a hard heat was coming back to I Corps and the ordeal at Khe Sanh was almost over. Flying across the westernmost stretches of the DMZ, you could read the history of that terrible winter just by looking at the hills.

For most of the time that the North Vietnamese had controlled Route 9 and kept the Marines isolated at Khe Sanh, all that anyone could see of the hills had been what little the transient mists allowed, a desolated terrain, cold, hostile, all colors deadened by the rainless monsoon or secreted in the fog. Now they were full and voluptuous in the new spring light.

Often you'd hear Marines talking about how beautiful those hills must have been, but that spring they were not beautiful. Once they had been the royal hunting grounds of the Annamese emperors. Tigers, deer and flying squirrels had lived in them. I used to imagine what a royal hunt must have been like, but I could only see it as an Oriental children's story: a conjuring of the emperor and empress, princes and princelings, court favorites and emissaries, all caparisoned for the hunt; slender figures across a tapestry, a promise of bloodless kills, a serene frolic complete with horseback flirtations and death-smiling game. And even now you could hear Marines comparing these hills with the hills around their homes, talking about what a pleasure it would be to hunt in them for anything other than men.

pouring out rays of bright, overturned earth all the way to the circumference; forms like Aztec sun figures, suggesting that their makers had been men who held Nature in an awesome reverence.

Once on a Chinook run from Cam Lo to Dong Ha, I sat next to a Marine who took a Bible from his pack and began reading even before we took off. He had a small cross sketched in ballpoint on his flak jacket and another, even less obtrusive, on his helmet cover. He was an odd-looking guy for a combat Marine in Vietnam. For one thing, he was never going to tan, no matter how many months he spent in the sun. He would just go red and blotchy, even though his hair was dark. He was also very heavy, maybe twenty pounds overweight, although you could see from his boots and fatigues that he'd humped it a lot over here. He wasn't a chaplain's assistant or anything, just a grunt who happened to be fat, pale and religious. (You didn't meet that many who were deeply religious, although you expected to, with so many kids from the South and the Midwest, from farms and small rural towns.) We strapped in and he started reading, getting very absorbed, and I leaned out the door and looked at the endless progression of giant pits which were splashed over the ground, at the acre-sized scars where napalm or chemical spray had eaten away the cover. (There was a special Air Force outfit that flew defoliation missions. They were called the Ranch Hands, and their motto was, "Only we can prevent forests.") When I held out some cigarettes to offer him one, he looked up from the Bible and shook his head, getting off that quick, pointless laugh that told me for sure that he'd seen a lot of action. Maybe he had even been at Khe Sanh, or up on 861 with 9th. I don't think he realized that I wasn't a Marine, I had on a Marine flak jacket

had plenty of helicopters, choppers were what the Cav was all about; and Sky Cranes lifted in earth-moving equipment, Chinooks brought in the heavier artillery pieces, and within days there was a forward operational base that looked better than most permanent installations in I Corps, complete with a thousand-meter airstrip and deep, ventilated bunkers. They named it LZ Stud, and once it was finished Khe Sanh ceased to be the center of its own sector; it became just another objective.

It was almost as though the war had ended. The day before Pegasus began, President Johnson had announced the suspension of airstrikes against the North and put a closing date on his own Administration. The Marines' 11th Engineers had begun moving down Route 9, deactivating mines and repairing bridges, and they had met with no resistance. The shelling of Khe Sanh had become a matter of a few scattered rounds a day, and it had been more than two weeks now since General Westmoreland had revealed that, in his opinion, the attack on Khe Sanh would never come. The 304th NVA Division had left the area, and so had the 325C. Now, it seemed that all but a token force of NVA had vanished. And now, everywhere you went, you could see the most comforting military insignia in all of Vietnam, the yellow-and-black shoulder patch of the Cav. You were with the pro's now, the elite. LZ's and firebases were being established at a rate of three and four a day, and every hour brought them closer to Khe Sanh.

Really, it was almost too good, and by the third day something odd attended Pegasus. As an operation, it revealed the tastes of the Cav's commander, Major General John Tolson, a general of uncommon intelligence and subtlety. Its precision and speed were unbelievable, especially to anyone who

had gone or why. Considering the amount of weapons and supplies being found (a record for the entire war), there were surprisingly few prisoners, although one prisoner did tell his interrogators that 75 percent of his regiment had been killed by our B-52's, nearly 1,500 men, and that the survivors were starving. He had been pulled out of a spider hole near Hill 881 North, and had seemed grateful for his capture. An American officer who was present at the interrogation actually said that the boy was hardly more than seventeen or eighteen, and that it was hideous that the North was feeding such young men into a war of aggression. Still, I don't remember anyone, Marine or Cav, officer or enlisted, who was not moved by the sight of their prisoners, by the sudden awareness of what must have been suffered and endured that winter.

For the first time in eleven weeks, Marines at Khe Sanh left their perimeter, walked two miles to Hill 471, and took it, after what amounted to the one serious battle of those weeks. (LZ's, including Stud, were sporadically rocketed and mortared; the Cav lost some ships to NVA gunners; there were small often sharp firefights almost every day. One or two body bags waited for removal at most landing zones on most afternoons, but it was different, and that was the trouble. After the slaughter of the winter, you were afraid of this unaccustomed mercy, afraid of becoming lax or afraid of having the Joke played on you. It was one thing, if it had to happen, to have it happen in Hue or Khe Sanh, but something else to be one of the few. WHY ME? was a common piece of helmet graffiti.) You'd hear a trooper of the Cav say something like, "I hear the Marines stepped into the shit above Route Nine," but what he really meant was, Of *course* the Marines stepped into the shit, what *else* would they be

it looked like heavy snow, and the ravines looked like ski trails.

He was from Alabama and he had all but decided on a career in the Army. Even before King's murder he had seen what this might someday mean, but he'd always hoped to get around it somehow.

"Now what I gonna do?" he said.

"I'm a great one to ask."

"But dig it. Am I gonna take 'n' turn them guns aroun' on my own people? Shit!"

That was it, there was hardly a black NCO anywhere who wasn't having to deal with that. We sat in the dark, and he told me that when he'd walked by me that afternoon it had made him sick. He couldn't help it.

"Shit, I can't do no twenty in this Army. They ain' no way. All's I hope is I can hang back when push comes t' shove. An' then I think, Well, fuck it, why should I? Man, home's just gonna be a hassle."

There was some firing on the hill, a dozen M-79 rounds and the dull bap-bap-bap of an AK-47, but that was over there, there was an entire American division between that and us. But the man was crying, trying to look away while I tried not to look.

"It's just a bad night for it," I said. "What can I tell you?"

He stood up, looked at the hill and then started to leave. "Oh, man," he said. "This war gets old."

At Langvei we found the two-month-old corpse of an American stretched out on the back of a wrecked jeep. This was on the top of the small hill that opposed the hill containing the Special Forces bunkers taken by the NVA in February. They were still in there, 700 meters away. The corpse was the worst thing we'd ever seen, utterly blackened now, the skin on the face drawn back tightly like

A rocket whistled by, missing the hill, and we ran for the bunkers. Two more came in, both missing, and then we moved out for the opposite hill one more time, watching the machine-gun slits for fluttering blips of light with one eye and checking the ground for booby traps with the other. But they had abandoned it during the night, and we took it without a shot, standing on top of the bunkers, looking down into Laos, past the remains of two bombed-out Russian tanks, feeling relieved, victorious and silly. When Merron and I flew back to Stud that afternoon, the two-month-old corpse rode with us. No one had covered him until ten minutes before the chopper had picked us up, and the body bag swarmed with flies until the motion of the rising chopper shook them off. We got out at Graves Registration with it, where one of the guys opened the bag and said, "Shit, this is a *gook!* What'd they bring him *here* for?"

"Look, Jesus, he's got on our uniform."

"I don't give a fuck, that ain't no American, that's a fucking *gook!*"

"Wait a minute," the other one said. "Maybe it's a spade. . . ."

The chopper that brought us back to Khe Sanh had barely touched the strip, and we were running again. I must have seen the Marines playing softball there, lounging around, hanging up laundry, but I rejected it and ran anyway. It was the only way I knew to behave there. I knew where the trench was, and went for it.

"Must be Airborne trainin'," some grunt called, and I slowed down.

"Ain' no hurry-up no more," a black Marine said. They all had their fatigue shirts off, there must have been hundreds of them, all around the field.

"I wouldn't say that."

Far up the strip, 400 meters away, there was a man sitting on some ammo crates. He was by himself. It was the colonel. I hadn't seen him in nearly six weeks, and he looked tired now. He had the same stare that the rest of the Marines here had, and the corners of his mustache had been rolled tortuously into two tight points that were caked with dried creamed coffee. Yes, he said, it sure would be good to get out of this place. He sat there looking at the hills, and I think that he was all but hypnotized by them now; they were not the same hills that had surrounded him for most of the past ten months. They had held such fearful mystery for so long that when they were suddenly found to be peaceful again, they were transformed as greatly as if a flood had swept over them.

A token American force was kept at Khe Sanh for the next month, and the Marines went back to patrolling the hills, as they had done a year before. A great many people wanted to know how the Khe Sanh Combat Base could have been the Western Anchor of our Defense one month and a worthless piece of ground the next, and they were simply told that the situation had changed. A lot of people suspected that some kind of secret deal had been made with the North; activity along the DMZ all but stopped after Khe Sanh was abandoned. The Mission called it a victory, and General Westmoreland said that it had been "a Dien Bien Phu in reverse." In early June engineers rolled up the airstrips and transported the salvaged tarmac back to Dong Ha. The bunkers were filled with high explosives and then blown up. The sandbagging and wire that remained were left to the jungle, which grew with a violence of energy now in the Highland

water and half in the sand. This was not the war for such images, you knew better, but they were Marines, and there was something terrible about seeing them there, limp in the wash of the tide.

Up from the beach there was a long, airless concrete building that served as a cafeteria. It had the best jukebox in Vietnam, and black Marines would spend more time there than on the beach, jiving around the room, carrying stacks of greasy hamburgers, dank french fries, giant paper cups full of malted milk, grape drink or (because it was so pretty, one of them told me) tomato juice. You'd sit at the tables there listening to the music, glad to be out of the sun, and every once in a while some grunts would recognize you from an operation and come over to talk. It was always nice to see them, but it always brought bad news, and sometimes the sight of what the war had done to them was awful. The two who came up to me now looked all right.

"You're a reporter, ain't you?"

I nodded.

"We seen you one time at Khe Sanh."

They were from the 26th Marines, Hotel Company, and they told me all about what had happened to the outfit since April. They weren't from the same platoon as Orrin and Day Tripper, but they knew that both of them had made it home. One of the guys who had run out to bring me a stretcher to sleep on was in a big hospital in Japan. I couldn't remember the name of the one grunt I most wanted to hear about, I was probably afraid of what they'd say, but I described him. He was a little cat with blond hair, and he was trying to grow a mustache.

"Oh, you mean Stoner."

"No, it wasn't that. He was always hanging out

Illumination Rounds

We were all strapped into the seats of the Chinook, fifty of us, and something, someone was hitting it from the outside with an enormous hammer. How do they do that? I thought, we're a thousand feet in the air! But it had to be that, over and over, shaking the helicopter, making it dip and turn in a horrible out-of-control motion that took me in the stomach. I had to laugh, it was so exciting, it was the thing I had wanted, almost what I had wanted except for that wrenching, resonant metal-echo; I could hear it even above the noise of the rotor blades. And they were going to fix that, I knew they would make it stop. They had to, it was going to make me sick.

They were all replacements going in to mop up after the big battles on Hills 875 and 876, the battles that had already taken on the name of one great battle, the battle of Dak To. And I was new, brand new, three days in-country, embarrassed about my boots because they were so new. And across from me, ten feet away, a boy tried to jump out of the straps and then jerked forward and hung there, his rifle barrel caught in the red plastic webbing of the seat back. As the chopper rose again and turned, his weight went back hard against the webbing and a dark spot the size of a baby's hand showed in the center of his fatigue jacket. And it grew—I knew what it was, but not really—it got up to his armpits and then started down his sleeves and up over his shoulders at the same time. It went all across his waist and down his legs, covering the

gotta go, you gotta go. All's I can say is, I hope you get a clean wound."

The battle for Hill 875 was over, and some survivors were being brought in by Chinook to the landing strip at Dak To. The 173rd Airborne had taken over 400 casualties, nearly 200 killed, all on the previous afternoon and in the fighting that had gone on all through the night. It was very cold and wet up there, and some girls from the Red Cross had been sent up from Pleiku to comfort the survivors. As the troops filed out of the helicopters, the girls waved and smiled at them from behind their serving tables. "Hi, soldier! What's your name?" "Where you from, soldier?" "I'll bet some hot coffee would hit the spot about now."

And the men from the 173rd just kept walking without answering, staring straight ahead, their eyes rimmed with red from fatigue, their faces pinched and aged with all that had happened during the night. One of them dropped out of line and said something to a loud, fat girl who wore a Peanuts sweatshirt under her fatigue blouse and she started to cry. The rest just walked past the girls and the large, olive-drab coffee urns. They had no idea of where they were.

A senior NCO in the Special Forces was telling the story: "We was back at Bragg, in the NCO Club, and this schoolteacher comes in an' she's real good-lookin'. Dusty here grabs her by the shoulders and starts runnin' his tongue all over her face like she's a fuckin' ice-cream cone. An' you know what she says? She says, 'I like you. You're different.' "

At one time they would have lighted your cigarette for you on the terrace of the Continental Hotel.

like before they'd made their arrangements with the engineers. You'd see them at the tables there, smiling their hard, empty smiles into those rangy, brutal, scared faces. No wonder those men all looked alike to the Vietnamese. After a while they all looked alike to me. Out on the Bien Hoa Highway, north of Saigon, there is a monument to the Vietnamese war dead, and it is one of the few graceful things left in the country. It is a modest pagoda set above the road and approached by long flights of gently rising steps. One Sunday, I saw a bunch of these engineers gunning their Harleys up those steps, laughing and shouting in the afternoon sun. The Vietnamese had a special name for them to distinguish them from all other Americans: it translated out to something like "The Terrible Ones," although I'm told that this doesn't even approximate the odium carried in the original.

There was a young sergeant in the Special Forces, stationed at the C Detachment in Can Tho, which served as the SF headquarters for IV Corps. In all, he had spent thirty-six months in Vietnam. This was his third extended tour, and he planned to come back again as soon as he possibly could after this current hitch was finished. During his last tour he had lost a finger and part of a thumb in a firefight, and he had been generally shot up enough times for the three Purple Hearts which mean that you don't have to fight in Vietnam anymore. After all that, I guess they thought of him as a combat liability, but he was such a hard charger that they gave him the EM Club to manage. He ran it well and seemed happy, except that he had gained a lot of weight in the duty, and it set him apart from the rest of the men. He loved to horse around with the Vietnamese in the compound, leaping on them from

me in and told me that I'd killed fourteen VC and liberated six prisoners. You want to see the medal?"

There was a little air-conditioned restaurant on the corner of Le Loi and Tu Do, across from the Continental Hotel and the old opera house which now served as the Vietnamese Lower House. Some of us called it the Graham Greene Milk Bar (a scene in *The Quiet American* had taken place there), but its name was Givral. Every morning they baked their own baguettes and croissants, and the coffee wasn't too bad. Sometimes, I'd meet there with a friend of mine for breakfast.

He was a Belgian, a tall, slow-moving man of thirty who'd been born in the Congo. He professed to know and love war, and he affected the mercenary sensibility. He'd been photographing the Vietnam thing for seven or eight years now, and once in a while he'd go over to Laos and run around the jungles there with the government, searching for the dreaded Pathet Lao, which he pronounced "Paddy Lao." Other people's stories of Laos always made it sound like a lotus land where no one wanted to hurt anyone, but he said that whenever he went on ops there he always kept a grenade taped to his belly because he was a Catholic and knew what the Paddy Lao would do to him if he were captured. But he was a little crazy that way, and tended to dramatize his war stories.

He always wore dark glasses, probably even during operations. His pictures sold to the wire services, and I saw a few of them in the American news magazines. He was very kind in a gruff, offhanded sort of way, kindness embarrased him, and he was so graceless among people, so eager to shock, that he couldn't understand why so many of us liked him.

"Father," the Marine said, "I'd like to ask you for something."

"What, son?"

"I'd like to have that cross." And he pointed to the tiny silver insignia on the chaplain's lapel.

"Of course," the chaplain said. "But why?"

"Well, it was the first thing I saw when I came to yesterday, and I'd like to have it."

The chaplain removed the cross and handed it to him. The Marine held it tightly in his fist and looked at the chaplain.

"You lied to me, Father," he said. "You cocksucker. You lied to me."

His name was Davies, and he was a gunner with a helicopter group based at Tan Son Nhut airport. On paper, by the regulations, he was billeted in one of the big "hotel" BEQ's in Cholon, but he only kept his things there. He actually lived in a small two-story Vietnamese house deeper inside of Cholon, as far from the papers and the regulations as he could get. Every morning he took an Army bus with wire-grille windows out to the base and flew missions, mostly around War Zone C, along the Cambodian border, and most nights he returned to the house in Cholon where he lived with his "wife" (whom he'd found in one of the bars) and some other Vietnamese who were said to be the girl's family. Her mamma-san and her brother were always there, living on the first floor, and there were others who came and went. He seldom saw the brother, but every few days he would find a pile of labels and brand names torn from cardboard cartons, American products that the brother wanted from the PX.

The first time I saw him he was sitting alone at a table on the Continental terrace, drinking a beer.

Jimi Hendrix, Dylan, Eldridge Cleaver, Rap Brown; coffins draped with American flags whose stars were replaced by swastikas and dollar signs; odd parts clipped from *Playboy* pictures, newspaper headlines (FARMERS BUTCHER HOGS TO PROTEST PORK PRICE DIP), photo captions (*President Jokes with Newsmen*), beautiful girls holding flowers, showers of peace symbols; Ky standing at attention and saluting, a small mushroom cloud forming where his genitalia should have been; a map of the western United States with the shape of Vietnam reversed and fitted over California and one large, long figure that began at the bottom with shiny leather boots and rouged knees and ascended in a microskirt, bare breasts, graceful shoulders and a long neck, topped by the burned, blackened face of a dead Vietnamese woman.

By the time Davies' friends showed up, we were already stoned. We could hear them below, laughing and rapping with Mama, and then they came up the stairs, three spades and two white guys.

"It sure do smell *peculiar* up here," one of them said.

"Hi, you freaky li'l fuckers."

"This grass is Number Ten," Davies said. "Every time I smoke this grass over here it gives me a bad trip."

"Ain' nuthin' th' matter with that grass," someone said. "It ain't the grass."

"Where's Hoa?"

"Yeah, Davies, where's your ole lady at?"

"She's out hustling Saigon tea, and I'm fucking sick of it." He tried to look really angry, but he only looked unhappy.

One of them handed off a joint and stretched out. "Hairy day today," he said.

"Where'd you fly?"

tards. So I just thought, What are they *really* like? and I came up with rinky-dink. Suits 'em just perfect, Rinky-Dink. 'Cept that was too long, so we cut it down some. And that's why we call 'em Dinks."

One morning before dawn, Ed Fouhy, a former Saigon bureau chief for CBS, went out to 8th Aerial Port at Tan Son Nhut to catch the early military flight to Danang. They boarded as the sun came up, and Fouhy strapped in next to a kid in rumpled fatigues, one of those soldiers you see whose weariness has gone far beyond physical exhaustion, into that state where no amount of sleep will ever give him the kind of rest he needs. Every torpid movement they make tells you that they are tired, that they'll stay tired until their tours are up and the big bird flies them back to the World. Their eyes are dim with it, their faces almost puffy, and when they smile you have to accept it as a token.

There was a standard question you could use to open a conversation with troops, and Fouhy tried it. "How long you been in-country?" he asked.

The kid half lifted his head; that question could *not* be serious. The weight was really on him, and the words came slowly.

"All fuckin' day," he said.

"You guys out to do a story on me suntahm," the kid said. He was a helicopter gunner, six-three with an enormous head that sat in bad proportion to the rest of his body and a line of picket teeth that were always on show in a wet, uneven smile. Every few seconds he would have to wipe his mouth with the back of his hand, and when he talked to you his face was always an inch from yours, so that I had to take my glasses off to keep them dry. He was

he was one of them. I didn't say anything, and then he said that he wasn't just a Panther; he was an agent for the Panthers, sent over here to recruit. I asked him what kind of luck he'd been having, and he said fine, real fine. There was a fierce wind blowing across the lz, and the joint didn't last very long.

"Hey, baby," he said, "that was just some shit I tol' you. Shit, I ain't no Panther. I was just fuckin' with you, see what you'd say."

"But the Panthers have guys over here. I've met some."

"Tha' could be," he said, and he laughed.

A Huey came in, and he jogged out to see where it was headed. It was going to Dak To, and he came back to get his gear. "Later, baby," he said. "An' luck." He jumped into the chopper, and as it rose from the strip he leaned out and laughed, bringing his arm up and bending it back toward him, palm out and the fist clenched tightly in the Sign.

One day I went out with the ARVN on an operation in the rice paddies above Vinh Long, forty terrified Vietnamese troops and five Americans, all packed into three Hueys that dropped us up to our hips in paddy muck. I had never been in a rice paddy before. We spread out and moved toward the marshy swale that led to the jungle. We were still twenty feet from the first cover, a low paddy wall, when we took fire from the treeline. It was probably the working half of a crossfire that had somehow gone wrong. It caught one of the ARVN in the head, and he dropped back into the water and disappeared. We made it to the wall with two casualties. There was no way of stopping their fire, no room to send a flanking party, so gunships were

The sergeant had lain out near the clearing for almost two hours with a wounded medic. He had called over and over for a medevac, but none had come. Finally, a chopper from another outfit, a LOH, appeared, and he was able to reach it by radio. The pilot told him that he'd have to wait for one of his own ships, they weren't coming down, and the sergeant told the pilot that if he did not land for them he was going to open fire from the ground and fucking well *bring* him down. So they were picked up that way, but there were repercussions.

The commander's code name was Mal Hombre, and he reached the sergeant later that afternoon from a place with the call signal Violent Meals.

"God *damn* it, Sergeant," he said through the static, "I thought you were a professional soldier."

"I waited as long as I could, Sir. Any longer, I was gonna lose my man."

"This outfit is perfectly capable of taking care of its own dirty laundry. Is that clear, Sergeant?"

"Colonel, since when is a wounded trooper 'dirty laundry'?"

"At ease, Sergeant," Mal Hombre said, and radio contact was broken.

There was a spec 4 in the Special Forces at Can Tho, a shy Indian boy from Chinle, Arizona, with large, wet eyes the color of ripe olives and a quiet way of speaking, a really nice way of putting things, kind to everyone without ever being stupid or soft about it. On the night that the compound and the airstrip were hit, he came and asked me if there was a chaplain anywhere around. He wasn't very religious, he said, but he was worried about tonight. He'd just volunteered for a "suicide squad," two jeeps that were going to drive across the air-

doctors had worked without a break, and now, on the second afternoon, the Viet Cong began shelling the hospital.

One of the Vietnamese nurses handed me a cold can of beer and asked me to take it down the hall where one of the Army surgeons was operating. The door of the room was ajar, and I walked right in. I probably should have looked first. A little girl was lying on the table, looking with wide dry eyes at the wall. Her left leg was gone, and a sharp piece of bone about six inches long extended from the exposed stump. The leg itself was on the floor, half wrapped in a piece of paper. The doctor was a major, and he'd been working alone. He could not have looked worse if he'd lain all night in a trough of blood. His hands were so slippery that I had to hold the can to his mouth for him and tip it up as his head went back. I couldn't look at the girl.

"Is it all right?" he said quietly.

"It's okay now. I expect I'll be sick as hell later on."

He placed his hand on the girl's forehead and said, "Hello, little darling." He thanked me for bringing the beer. He probably thought that he was smiling, but nothing changed anywhere in his face. He'd been working this way for nearly twenty hours.

The Intel report lay closed on the green field table, and someone had scrawled "What does it all mean?" across the cover sheet. There wasn't much doubt about who had done that; the S-2 was a known ironist. There were so many like him, really young captains and majors who had the wit to cut back their despair, a wedge to set against the bitterness. What got to them sooner or later was an

was still cool, but heavy, too, as though a terrible heat was coming on. The major and I stood by the tent and watched while an F-4 flew nose-down, released its load against the base of a hill, leveled and flew upward again.

"I've been having this dream," the major said. "I've had it two times now. I'm in a big examination room back at Quantico. They're handing out questionnaires for an aptitude test. I take one and look at it, and the first question says, 'How many kinds of animals can you kill with your hands?' "

We could see rain falling in a sheet about a kilometer away. Judging by the wind, the major gave it three minutes before it reached us.

"After the first tour, I'd have the goddamndest nightmares. You know, the works. Bloody stuff, bad fights, guys dying, *me* dying . . . I thought they were the worst," he said. "But I sort of miss them now."

Colleagues

I

There's a candle end burning in a corner of the bunker, held to the top of a steel helmet by melted wax, the light guttering over a battered typewriter, and the Old Guy is getting one off: "Tat-tat-tat, tatta-tatta-tat like your kid or your brother or your sweetheart maybe never wanted much for himself never asked for anything except for what he knew to be his some men have a name for it and they call it Courage when the great guns are still at last across Europe what will it matter maybe after all that this one boy from Cleveland Ohio won't becoming back-a-tat-tat." You can hear shellfire landing just outside, a little gravel falls into the typewriter, but the candle burns on, throwing its faint light over the bowed head and the few remaining wisps of white hair. Two men, the Colonel and the Kid, stand by the door watching. "Why, Sir?" the Kid asks. "What makes him do it? He could be sitting safe in London right now." "I don't know, son," the Colonel says. "Maybe he figures he's got a job to do, too. Maybe it's because he's somebody who really cares. . . ."

I never knew a member of the Vietnam press corps who was insensible to what happened when the words "war" and "correspondent" got joined. The glamour of it was possibly empty and lunatic, but there were times when it was all you had, a benign

was waiting to get on a helicopter, a long wait with all of the dead and badly wounded going out first, and a couple of sniper rounds snapped across the airstrip, forcing us to move behind some sandbagging. "I *hate* this movie," he said, and I thought, "Why not?") My movie, my friends, my colleagues. But meet them in context:

There was a ridge called Mutter's Ridge that ran the crest of one of those DMZ hills which the Americans usually named according to height in meters, Hill Three Hundred Whatever. The Marines had been up there since early morning, when Kilo Company and four correspondents were choppered into a sparse landing zone on the highest rise of the ridge. If this had been an Army operation, we would have been digging now, correspondents too, but the Marines didn't do that, their training taught them more about fatal gesture than it did about survival. Everyone was saying that Charlie was probably just over there on the next hill scoping on us, but the grunts were keeping it all in the open, walking out along the ridge "coordinating," setting up positions and cutting out a proper lz with battery-powered saws and chunks of explosive. Every few minutes one or another of them would shag down to the spot below the lz where the correspondents were sitting and warn us indifferently about the next blast, saying. "Uh, listen, there's fire in the hole, so you guys wanna just turn your backs and sort of cover over your heads?" He'd hang in there for a moment to give us a good look, and then run back up to the lz site to tell the others about us.

"Hey, see them four guys there? Them're reporters."

"Bullshit, reporters."

It was one thing for a lone reporter to join an outfit before an operation because the outfit, if it was a company or larger, could absorb him and the curiosity that his presence always set working, and when the operation was over most of the troops would never even know that he'd been along. But when six correspondents turned up on the eve of an operation, especially when it fell during a long period of light contact, the effect was so complicated that the abiding ambivalence of all troops and commanders toward all reporters didn't even begin to explain it. Everyone from the colonel to the lowest-ranking grunt felt a new importance about what he was going into, and to all appearances, as far as they were in touch with it, they were glad to see you. But our presence was also unnerving, picking at layers of fear that they might never have known about otherwise. ("Why us? I mean, *six* of those bastards, where the hell are we *going?*") When it came all the way down to this, even the poorest-connected free-lancer had the power on him, a power which only the most pompous and unfeeling journalists ever really wanted, throwing weird career scares into the staff and laying a cutting edge against each Marine's gut estimates of his own survival. Then, it didn't matter that we were dressed exactly as they were and would be going exactly where they were going; we were as exotic and as fearsome as black magic, coming on with cameras and questions, and if we promised to take the anonymity off of what was about to happen, we were also there to watchdog the day. The very fact that we had chosen *them* seemed to promise the most awful kind of engagement, because they were all certain that war correspondents never wasted time. It was a joke we all dug.

wait while a dozen men got out and walked around the perimeter, "like they was just checking things out"). It had been a mild season for Vietnam correspondents too (the lull aside, home offices were beginning to make it clear to their Saigon bureaus that the story was losing the old bite, what with Johnson's abdication, the spring assassinations and the coming elections), and we were either talking about how the Vietnam thing was really finished or bitching about getting shot at only to wind up on page nine. It was a good time to cruise the country, a day here and a week there, just hanging out with troops; a good time to make leisurely investigations into the smaller, darker pockets of the war. Now word had come down that a large mass of NVA was moving across the DMZ, possibly building for a new offensive against Hue, and battalions of the 5th Marines were deploying in rough conjunction with batallions of the 9th to find and kill them. It had the feel of what we always called a "good operation," and the six of us had gone up for it.

But there was nothing here now, no dreaded Cong, no shelling, no pictures for the wires, no stories for the files, no sign that anyone had been on this scalding ridge for at least six months. (A few miles north and a little east, a company of the 9th was in the middle of an evil firefight that would last until nightfall, leaving eleven of them dead and nearly thirty wounded, but we knew nothing about that now. If we had, we might possibly have made an effort at getting to it, some of us at least, explaining it later in cold professional terms and leaving all the other reasons unspoken, understood between us. If a Marine had ever expressed a similar impulse, we would probably have called him psychotic.) The only violence

that didn't mean much to the grunts since most of them, the young ones, had barely even heard of Errol Flynn. It was just apparent to anyone who looked at him that he was what the Marines would call "a dude who definitely had his shit together." All four of us on the ridge looked more or less as though we belonged there; the AP's John Lengle had covered every major Marine operation of the past eighteen months, Nick Wheeler of UPI had been around for two years, I'd had the better part of a year in now, we were all nearly young enough to be mistaken for grunts ourselves, but Flynn was special. We all had our movie-fed war fantasies, the Marines too, and it could be totally disorienting to have this outrageously glamorous figure intrude on them, really unhinging, like looking up to see that you've been sharing a slit trench with John Wayne or William Bendix. But you got used to that part of Flynn quickly.

When he'd first arrived in Vietnam in the summer of 1965, he had been considered news himself and a lot of stories were written about his early trips into combat. Most of them managed to include all the clichés, all of them called him "swashbuckling." There were still a lot of easy things to say about him, and a lot of people around who were more than willing to say them, but after you knew him all of that talk just depressed you. There were a number of serious (heavy) journalists who could not afford to admit that anyone who looked as good as Flynn looked could possibly have anything more going for him. They chose not to take his as seriously as they took themselves (which was fine with Sean), and they accused him of coming to Vietnam to play, as though the war was like Africa had been for him, or the South of France or one of the places he'd gone to make those

It was still a little too soon for the Marines to just sit down and start talking, they would have to probe a little more first, and we were getting bored. By the time they had finished cutting the lz there was no cover left from the sun, and we were all anxious for the scouting platoon to reach the top so that we could get together with Dana Stone, put a little pressure on for a helicopter and get out. The trip back to the press center in Danang could take two hours or two days, depending on what was flying, but it was certain to go faster with Stone along because he had friends at every airfield and chopper pad in I Corps. Danang was Soul City for many of us, it had showers and drinks, flash-frozen air-freighted steaks, air-conditioned rooms and China Beach and, for Stone, a real home—a wife, a dog, a small house full of familiar possessions. Mutter's Ridge had sickening heat, a rapidly vanishing water supply and boredom, so there really wasn't any choice. Judging by the weathered, blackened bits of ammunition casing (theirs and ours) that littered the ground around us, the ridge also had a history, and Dana had told us something about it.

Stone was a lapsed logger from Vermont (he always spoke about going back to that, especially after a bad day in the field, screw all this bullshit), twenty-five years old with sixty-year-old eyes set in deep behind wire-rimmed glasses, their shrewdness and experience almost lost in the lean anglings of his face. We knew for certain that he would be walking well ahead of the rest of the platoon on the trail, standard Dana and a break for the Marines, since he was easily the best equipped man in the party for spotting booby traps or ambushes. But that had nothing to do with his being on point. Dana was the man in motion, he just

with the 9th that time, and they'd *really stepped in deep shit.* (It was true, we all knew it was true, he was doing it to us again, and a smile showed for just an instant on his face.) They had been pinned down on the ridge all night long without support or re-supply or medevac, and the *casualties* had been *unbelievable,* running somewhere around 70 percent. Flynn laughed and said, "Dana, you bastard," but Stone would have gone on like that in his flat Vermont voice, telling it to those of us about to go up there as though it were nothing more than the history of a racehorse, except that he looked up and saw that we weren't alone; a few of the guys from Kilo Company had come over to ask questions about our cameras or something, and they'd heard some of it. Stone turned a deep red, as he always did when he realized that he'd gone a little too far. "Aw, that was just a bunch of shit, I never even been *near* that ridge," he said, and pointed to me. "I was just trying to get him uptight because this is his last operation, and he's already fucked up about it." He laughed, but he was looking at the ground.

Now, while we waited for him, a Marine came up to Lengle and me and asked if we'd like to look at some pictures he'd taken. Marines felt comfortable around Lengle, who looked like a college basketball star, six-seven and very young (actually, he was thirty), a Nevadan who'd parlayed a nice-kid image into a valuable professional asset. The pictures were in a little imitation-leather folder, and you could tell by the way the Marine stood over us, grinning in anticipation as we flipped over each plastic page, that it was among his favorite things. (He'd also taken some "number-one souvenirs," he said, leaving the details to our imaginations.) There were hundreds of these albums in

Stars and Stripes. You think the *Stripes* would run 'em?"

"Well . . ." We were laughing now, what could you do? Half the combat troops in Vietnam had these things in their packs, snapshots were the least of what they took after a fight, at least pictures didn't rot. I'd talked to a Marine who'd taken a lot of pictures after an operation on the Cua Viet River, and later, when he was getting short and nervous about things, he'd brought them to the chaplain. But the chaplain had only told him that it was forgivable and put the pictures in his drawer and kept them.

A couple of Marines were talking to Flynn and Wheeler about their cameras, the best place to buy this lens, the right speed to use for that shot, I couldn't follow any of it. The grunts were hip enough to the media to take photographers more seriously than reporters, and I'd met officers who refused to believe that I was really a correspondent because I never carried cameras. (During a recent operation, this had almost gotten me bumped from the Command chopper because the colonel, for reasons of his own, was partial to photographers. On that one, a company of his battalion had made contact with a company of Viet Cong and forced them out on a promontory, holding them there between their fire and the sea for the gunships to kill. This particular colonel loved to order the chopper in very low so that he could fire his .45 into the Cong, and he'd always wanted pictures of it. He was doubly disappointed that day; I'd not only turned up without a camera, but by the time we got there all the VC were dead, about 150 of them littered across the beach and bobbing in and out with the waves. But he fired off a few clips anyway, just to keep his piece working.)

said, looking really puzzled. "You mean you guys *volunteer* to come over here?"

"Well, dumb shit, what'd you think?" the Avenger said. "You think they're just some dumb grunt like you?"

"Oh man, you *got* to be kidding me. You guys *asked* to come here?"

"Sure."

"How long do you have to stay?" he asked.

"As long as we want."

"Wish *I* could stay as long as *I* want," the Marine called Love Child said. *"I'd* been home las' March."

"When did you get here?" I asked.

"Las' March."

The lieutenant who had been supervising the blasting looked down from the lz and yelled for someone named Collins.

"Yes Sir?" the Avenger said.

"Collins, get your bod up here."

"Yes Sir."

There was some movement on the lz now, the platoon had reached the clearing. Stone came out first, backing out very fast with his camera up, referring quickly to the ground just behind him between shots. Four Marines came out next, carrying a fifth on an improvised litter. They brought him to the center of the clearing and set him down carefully on the grass. We thought at first that he was dead, taken off by a booby trap on the trail, but his color was much too awful for that. Even the dead held some horrible light that seemed to recede, vanishing through one layer of skin at a time and taking a long time to go completely, but this kid had no color about him anywhere. It was incredible that anything so motionless and white could still be alive.

the matter with that man, feed some salt into him, get him up, get him walking, this is the Marines, not the goddamned Girl Scouts, there won't be any damned chopper coming in *here* today. (The four of us must have looked a little stricken at this, and Dana took our picture. We were really pulling for the kid; if he stayed, we stayed, and that meant all night.) The corpsmen were trying to tell the colonel that this was no ordinary case of heat exhaustion, excusing themselves but staying firm about it, refusing to let the colonel return to the CP. (The four of us smiled and Dana took a picture. "Go away, Stone," Flynn said. "'Hold it just like that," Stone said, running in for a closeup so that his lens was an inch away from Flynn's nose. "One more.") The Marine looked awful lying there, trying to work his lips a little, and the colonel glared down at the fragile, still form as though it was blackmailing him. When the Marine refused to move anything except his lips for fifteen minutes, the colonel began to relent. He asked the corpsmen if they'd ever heard of a man dying from something like this.

"Oh, yes Sir. Oh, wow, I mean he really needs more attention than what we can give him here."

"Mmmmmm . . ." the colonel said. Then he authorized the chopper request and strode with what I'm sure he considered great determination back to his CP.

"I think it would have made him feel better if he could have shot the kid," Flynn said.

"Or one of us," I said.

"You're just lucky he didn't get you last night," Flynn said. The evening before, when Flynn and I had arrived together at the base camp, the colonel had taken us into the Command bunker to show us some maps and explain the operation, and a

It was a Marine, and as soon as I saw him I realized that I'd seen him before, a minute or so ago, standing on the edge of the clearing staring at us as we got ourselves ready to leave. He'd been with a lot of Marines there, but I'd seen him much more distinctly than the others without realizing or admitting it. The others had been looking at us too, with amusement or curiosity or envy (we were splitting, casualties and correspondents this way out, we were going to Danang), they were all more or less friendly, but this one was different, I'd seen it, known it and passed it over, but not really. He was walking by us now, and I saw that he had a deep, running blister that seemed to have opened and eaten away much of his lower lip. That wasn't the thing that had made him stand out before, though. If I'd noticed it at all, it might have made him seem more wretched than the others, but nothing more. He stopped for a second and looked at us, and he smiled some terrifying, evil smile, his looked turned now to the purest hatred.

"You fucking guys," he said. "You guys are *crazy?*"

There was the most awful urgency to the way he said it. He was still glaring, I expected him to raise a finger and touch each of us with destruction and decay, and I realized that after all this time, the war still offered at least one thing that I had to turn my eyes from. I had seen it before and hoped never to see it again, I had misunderstood it and been hurt by it, I thought I had finally worked it out for good and I was looking at it now, knowing what it meant and feeling as helpless under it this last time as I had the first.

All right, yes, it had been a groove being a war correspondent, hanging out with the grunts and getting close to the war, touching it, losing yourself in

enough feeling left to say, "Okay, man, you go on, you go on out of here you cocksucker, but I mean it, you tell it! You tell it, man. If you don't tell it . . ."

What a time they were having there, it had all broken down, one battalion had taken 60 percent casualties, all the original NCO's were gone, the grunts were telling their officers to go die, to go fuck themselves, to go find some other fools to run up those streets awhile, it was no place where I'd have to tell anyone not to call me "Sir." They understood that, they understood a lot more than I did, but nobody hated me there, not even when I was leaving. Three days later I came back and the fighting had dropped off, the casualties were down to nothing and the same Marine flashed me a victory sign that had nothing to do with the Marine Corps or the fading battle or the American flag that had gone up on the Citadel's south wall the day before, he slapped me on the back and poured me a drink from a bottle he'd found in one of the hootches somewhere. Even the ones who preferred not to be in your company, who despised what your work required or felt that you took your living from their deaths, who believed that all of us were traitors and liars and the creepiest kinds of parasites, even they would cut back at the last and make their one concession to what there was in us that we ourselves loved most: "I got to give it to you, you guys got balls." Maybe they meant just that and nothing more, we had our resources and we made enough out of that to keep us going, turning the most grudging admissions into decorations for valor, making it all all right again.

But there was often that bad, bad moment to recall, the look that made you look away, and in its hateful way it was the purest single thing I'd

II

Name me someone that's not a parasite,
And I'll go out and say a prayer for him.
—BOB DYLAN, "Visions of Johanna"

I keep thinking about all the kids who got wiped out by seventeen years of war movies before coming to Vietnam to get wiped out for good. You don't know what a media freak is until you've seen the way a few of those grunts would run around during a fight when they knew that there was a television crew nearby; they were actually making war movies in their heads, doing little guts-and-glory Leatherneck tap dances under fire, getting their pimples shot off for the networks. They were insane, but the war hadn't done that to them. Most combat troops stopped thinking of the war as an adventure after their first few firefights, but there were always the ones who couldn't let that go, these few who were up there doing numbers for the cameras. A lot of correspondents weren't much better. We'd all seen too many movies, stayed too long in Television City, years of media glut had made certain connections difficult. The first few times that I got fired at or saw combat deaths, nothing really happened, all the responses got locked in my head. It was the same familiar violence, only moved over to another medium; some kind of jungle play with giant helicopters and fantastic special effects, actors lying out there in canvas body bags waiting for the scene to end so they could get up again and walk it off. But that was some scene (you found out), there was no cutting it.

400 meters up that street, and we knew that the entire way was open to sniper fire, either from the standing sections of the wall on our right or from the rooftops on our left. When we'd run to our present position an hour earlier, David had gone first, and it was my turn now. We were crouching among some barren shrubbery with the Marines, and I turned to the guy next to me, a black Marine, and said, "Listen, we're going to cut out now. Will you cover us?" He gave me one of those amazed, penetrating looks. "You can go out there if you want to, baby, but shee-it . . ." and he began putting out fire. David and I ran all doubled over, taking cover every forty meters or so behind boulder-sized chunks of smashed wall, and halfway through it I started to laugh, looking at David and shaking my head. David was the most urbane of correspondents, a Bostonian of good family and impeccable education, something of a patrician even though he didn't care anything about it. We were pretty good friends, and he was willing to take my word for it that there was actually something funny, and he laughed too.

"What is it?" he said.

"Oh man, do you realize that I just asked that guy back there to *cover us?*"

He looked at me with one eyebrow faintly cocked. "Yes," he said. "Yes, you did. Oh, isn't that *marvelous!*"

And we would have laughed all the way up the street, except that toward the end of it we had to pass a terrible thing, a house that had been collapsed by the bombing, bringing with it a young girl who lay stretched out dead on top of some broken wood. The whole thing was burning, and the flames were moving closer and closer to her bare feet. In a few minutes they were going to reach her, and

vague. I wasn't really an oddity in the press corps, but I was a peculiarity, an extremely privileged one. (An oddity was someone like the photographer John Schneider, who fixed a white flag to his handlebars and took a bike from the top of Hill 881 North over to Hill 881 South during a terrible battle, in what came to be known as Schneider's Ride; or the Korean cameraman who had spent four years in Spain as a matador, who spoke exquisite, limpid Castilian and whom we called El Taikwando; or the Portuguese novelist who arrived at Khe Sanh in sports clothes, carrying a plaid suitcase, under the impression that field gear could be bought there.)

I'd run into Bernie Weinraub in Saigon, on his way to *The New York Times* bureau carrying a bunch of papers in his hand. He'd be coming back from a meeting with some of "the beautiful people" of the Joint U.S. Public Affairs Office, and he'd say, "I'm having a low-grade nervous breakdown right now. You can't really see it, but it's there. After you've been here awhile, you'll start having them too," laughing at the little bit of it that was true as much as at the part of it that had become our running joke. Between the heat and the ugliness and the pressures of filing, the war out there and the JUSPAO flacks right here, Saigon could be overwhelmingly depressing, and Bernie often looked possessed by it, so gaunt and tired and underfed that he could have brought out the Jewish mother in a Palestinian guerrilla.

"Let's have a drink," I'd say.

"No, no, I can't. You know how it is, we on the *Times* . . ." He'd start to laugh. "I mean, *we* have to file every day. It's a terrible responsibility, there's so little time. . . . I hope you'll understand."

"Of course. I'm sorry, I just wasn't thinking."

that rode us into attrition traps on the back of fictional kill ratios, and an Administration that believed the Command, a cross-fertilization of ignorance, and a press whose tradition of objectivity and fairness (not to mention self-interest) saw that all of it got space. It was inevitable that once the media took the diversions seriously enough to report them, they also legitimized them. The spokesmen spoke in words that had no currency left as words, sentences with no hope of meaning in the sane world, and if much of it was sharply queried by the press, all of it got quoted. The press got all the facts (more or less), it got too many of them. But it never found a way to report meaningfully about death, which of course was really what it was all about. The most repulsive, transparent gropes for sanctity in the midst of the killing received serious treatment in the papers and on the air. The jargon of Progress got blown into your head like bullets, and by the time you waded through all the Washington stories and all the Saigon stories, all the Other War stories and the corruption stories and the stories about brisk new gains in ARVN effectiveness, the suffering was somehow unimpressive. And after enough years of that, so many that it seemed to have been going on forever, you got to a point where you could sit there in the evening and listen to the man say that American casualties for the week had reached a six-week low, only eighty GI's had died in combat, and you'd feel like you'd just gotten a bargain.

If you ever saw stories written by Peter Kann, William Touhy, Tom Buckley, Bernie Weinraub, Peter Arnett, Lee Lescaze, Peter Braestrup, Charles Mohr, Ward Just or a few others, you'd know that most of what the Mission wanted to say to the American public was a psychotic vaudeville;

renewed, I never had to frequent JUSPAO unless I wanted to. (That office had been created to handle press relations and psychological warfare, and I never met anyone there who seemed to realize that there was a difference.) I could skip the daily briefings, I never had to cultivate Sources. In fact, my concerns were so rarefied that I had to ask other correspondents what they ever found to ask Westmoreland, Bunker, Komer and Zorthian. (Barry Zorthian was the head of JUSPAO; for more than five years he *was* Information.) What did anybody ever expect those people to *say?* No matter how highly placed they were, they were still officials, their views were well established and well known, famous. It could have rained frogs over Tan Son Nhut and they wouldn't have been upset; Cam Ranh Bay could have dropped into the South China Sea and they would have found some way to make it sound good for you; the Bo Doi Division (Ho's Own) could have marched by the American embassy and they would have characterized it as "desperate"—what did even the reporters closest to the Mission Council ever find to write about when they'd finished their interviews? (My own interview with General Westmoreland had been hopelessly awkward. He'd noticed that I was accredited to *Esquire* and asked me if I planned to be doing "humoristical" pieces. Beyond that, very little was really said. I came away feeling as though I'd just had a conversation with a man who touches a chair and says, "This is a chair," points to a desk and says, "This is a desk." I couldn't think of anything to ask him, and the interview didn't happen.) I honestly wanted to know what the form was for those interviews, but some of the reporters I'd ask would get very officious, saying something about "Command postures," and look at me as though I

those long night gatherings in Saigon, the ashtrays heaped over, ice buckets full of warm water, bottles empty, the grass all gone, the words running, "You know I watch that rotten box until my head begin to hurt, From checkin' out the way the newsmen say they get the dirt" (bitter funny looks passing around the room), "And if another woman driver gets machine-gunned from her seat, They'll send some joker with a Brownie and you'll see it all complete" (lip-biting, flinching, nervous laughter), "And if the place blows up, we'll be the first to tell, 'Cause the boys we got downtown are workin' hard and doin' swell . . ." That wasn't really about *us*, no, we were *so* hip, and we'd laugh and wince every time we heard it, all of us, wire-service photographers and senior correspondents from the networks and special-assignment types like myself, all grinning together because of what we knew together, that in the back of every column of print you read about Vietnam there was a dripping, laughing death-face; it hid there in the newspapers and magazines and held to your television screens for hours after the set was turned off for the night, an after-image that simply wanted to tell you at last what somehow had not been told.

On an afternoon shortly before the New Year, a few weeks before Tet, a special briefing was held in Saigon to announce the latest revisions in the hamlet-rating system of the Pacification program, the A-B-C-D profiling of the country's security and, by heavy inference, of the government's popular support "in the countryside," which meant any place outside of Saigon, the boonies. A lot of correspondents went, many because they had to, and I spent the time with a couple of photographers in one of the bars on Tu Do, talking to some soldiers from the 1st Infantry Division who had

signed to the department of JUSPAO which issued those little plastic-coated MACV accreditation cards. He'd hand them out and add their number to a small blackboard on the wall and then stare at the total in amused wonder, telling you that he thought it was all a fucking circus. (He's the same man who told a television star, "Hold on to your ass awhile. You people from the electronic media don't scare me anymore.") There was nothing exclusive about that card or its operational match, the Bao Chi credential of the Republic of South Vietnam; thousands of them must have been issued over the years. All they did was admit you to the Vietnam press corps and tell you that you could go out and cover the war if you really wanted to. All kinds of people have held them at one time or another: feature writers for religious organs and gun magazines, summer vacationers from college newspapers (one paper sent two, a Hawk and a Dove, and we put it down because it hadn't sent a Moderate over as well), second-string literary figures who wrote about how they hated the war more than you or I ever could, syndicated eminences who houseguested with Westmoreland or Bunker and covered operations in the presence of Staff, privileges which permitted them to chronicle fully our great victory at Tet, and to publish evidence year after year after year that the back of the Cong had been broken, Hanoi's will dissolved. There was no nation too impoverished, no hometown paper so humble that it didn't get its man in for a quick feel at least once. The latter tended to be the sort of old reporter that most young reporters I knew were afraid of becoming someday. You'd run into them once in a while at the bar of the Danang press center, men in their late forties who hadn't had the chance to slip into uniform

perience had been shooting fashion, Koreans who were running PX privileges into small fortunes, Japanese who trailed so many wires that transistor jokes were inevitable, Vietnamese who took up combat photography to avoid the draft, Americans who spent all their days in Saigon drinking at the bar of L'Amiral Restaurant with Air America pilots. Some filed nothing but hometowners, some took the social notes of the American community, some went in the field only because they couldn't afford hotels, some never left their hotels. Taken all together, they accounted for most of the total on Gunny's blackboard, which left a number of people, as many as fifty, who were gifted or honest or especially kind and who gave journalism a better name than it deserved, particularly in Vietnam. Finally, the press corps was as diffuse and faceless as any regiment in the war, the main difference being that many of us remained on our own orders.

It was a characteristic of a lot of Americans in Vietnam to have no idea of when they were being obscene, and some correspondents fell into that, writing their stories from the daily releases and battlegrams, tracking them through with the cheer-crazed language of the MACV Information Office, things like "discreet burst" (one of those tore an old grandfather and two children to bits as they ran along a paddy wall one day, at least according to the report made later by the gunship pilot), "friendly casualties" (not warm, not fun), "meeting engagement" (ambush), concluding usually with 17 or 117 or 317 enemy dead and American losses "described as light." There were correspondents who had the same sensibility concerning the dead as the Command had: Well, in a war you've got to expect a little mud to get tracked over the carpet, we took a real black eye but we sure gave Charlie

came indistinguishable, others standing in contemptuous opposition to one another; and it was far too small to incorporate the whole bloated, amorphous body of the Vietnam press corps. Its requirements were unstated because, other than sensibility and style, it had none. Elsewhere, it would have been just another scene, another crowd, but the war gave it urgency and made it a deep thing, so deep that we didn't even have to like one another to belong. There was a lot that went unsaid at the time, but just because it was seldom spoken didn't mean that we weren't very much aware of it or that, in that terrible, shelterless place, we weren't grateful for each other.

It made room for correspondents who were themselves members of Saigon's American Establishment, it included young marrieds, all kinds of girl reporters, a lot of Europeans, the Ivy-League-in-Asia crowd, the Danang bunch, the Straights and the Heads, formals and funkies, old hands (many of whom were very young) and even some tourists, people who wanted to go somewhere to screw around for a while and happened to choose the war. There was no way of thinking about "who we were" because we were all so different, but where we were alike we were really alike. It helped if you went out on operations a lot or if you were good at your work, but neither was very necessary as long as you knew something of what the war was (as opposed to what the Mission and MACV told you it was), and as long as you weren't a snob about it. We were all doing terribly upsetting work, it could often be very dangerous, and we were the only ones who could tell, among ourselves, whether that work was any good. Applause from home meant nothing next to a nice word from a colleague. (One reporter loved to call his New York

towns. You could make friends elsewhere, a Special Forces captain in the Delta, a grunt up in Phu Bai, some decent, witty (and usually suffering) member of the Embassy Political Section. But whether you hung out with them or with other correspondents, all you ever talked about anyway was the war, and they could come to seem like two very different wars after a while. Because who but another correspondent could talk the kind of mythical war that you wanted to hear described? (Just hearing the way Flynn pronounced the word "Vietnam," the tenderness and respect that he put in it, taught you more about the beauty and horror of the place than anything the apologists or explainers could ever teach you.) Who could you discuss politics with, except a colleague? (We all had roughly the same position on the war: we were in it, and that was a position.) Where else could you go for a real sense of the war's past? There were all kinds of people who knew the background, the facts, the most minute details, but only a correspondent could give you the exact mood that attended each of the major epochs: the animal terror of the Ia Drang or the ghastly breakdown of the first major Marine operation, code-named Starlight, where the Marines were dying so incredibly fast, so far beyond the Command's allowance, that one of them got zipped into a body bag and tossed to the top of a pile of KIA's while he was still alive. He regained consciousness up there and writhed and heaved until his bag rolled to the ground, where some corpsmen found him and saved him. The Triangle and Bong Son were as remote as the Reservoir or Chickamauga, you had to hear the history from somebody you could trust, and who else could you trust? And if you saw some piece of helmet graffiti that seemed to say everything, you weren't going

were together on one of the lz's that had been built for the operation that was supposedly relieving Khe Sanh, and Burrows had run down to take pictures of a Chinook that was coming in to land. The wind was strong enough to send tarmac strips flying fifty feet across the lz and he ran through it to work, photographing the crew, getting the soldiers coming down the incline to board the chopper, getting the kids throwing off the mailbags and cartons of rations and ammunition, getting the three wounded being lifted carefully on board, turning again to get the six dead in their closed body bags, then the rise of the chopper (the wind now was strong enough to tear papers out of your hand), photographing the grass blown flat all around him and the flying debris, taking one picture each of the chopper rearing, settling and departing. When it was gone he looked at me, and he seemed to be in the most open distress. "Sometimes one feels like such a bastard," he said.

And that was one more thing we shared. We had no secrets about it or the ways it could make you feel. We all talked about it at times, some talked about it too much, a few never seemed to talk about anything else. That was a drag, but it was all in the house; you only minded it when it came from outside. All kinds of thieves and killers managed to feel sanctimonious around us; battalion commanders, civilian businessmen, even the grunts, until they realized how few of us were making any real money in it. There's no way around it, if you photographed a dead Marine with a poncho over his face and got something for it, you were *some* kind of parasite. But what were you if you pulled the poncho back first to make a better shot, and did that in front of his friends? Some other kind of parasite, I suppose. Then what were you if you

as you could have, it could have been closer without your even knowing it, like an early-morning walk I took once from the hilltop position of a Special Forces camp where I'd spent the night, down to the teamhouse at the foot of the hill, where I was going to have some coffee. I walked off the main trail onto a smaller trail and followed it until I saw the house and a group of eight giggling, wide-eyed Vietnamese mercenaries, Mikes, pointing at me and talking very excitedly. They all grabbed for me at once when I reached the bottom, and as it was explained to me a moment later, I'd just come down a trail which the Special Forces had rigged out with more than twenty booby traps, any one of which could have taken me off. (Any One Of Which ran through my head for days afterward.) If you went out often, just as surely as you'd eventually find yourself in a position where survival etiquette insisted that you take a weapon ("You know how this thang works 'n' airthang?" a young sergeant had to ask me once, and I'd had to nod as he threw it to me and said, "Then git some!", the American banzai), it was unavoidable that you'd find yourself almost getting killed. You expected something like that to happen, but not exactly that, not until events made things obvious for you. A close call was like a loss of noncombatant status: you weren't especially proud of it, you merely reported it to a friend and then stopped talking about it, knowing in the first place that the story would go around from there, and that there wasn't really anything to be said about it anyway. But that didn't stop you from thinking about it a lot, doing a lot of hideous projecting from it, forming a system of pocket metaphysics around it, getting it down to where you found yourself thinking about which *kind* of thing was closer: that walk down the

like an animal into the crowds of Cholon. He said that they had all yelled, "Bao Chi!" a number of times, but that they had been machine-gunned anyway.

It was more like death by misadventure than anything else, as if that mattered, and of the four dead correspondents, only one had been a stranger. Two of the others were good acquaintances, and the fourth was a friend. His name was John Cantwell, an Australian who worked for *Time*, and he had been one of the first friends I'd made in Vietnam. He was a kind, congenial mock-goat whose talk was usually about the most complex, unimaginable lecheries, architectural constructions of monumental erotic fantasies. He had a Chinese wife and two children in Hong Kong (he spoke fluent Chinese, he'd take it through the Cholon bars for us sometimes), and he was one of the few I knew who really hated Vietnam and the war, every bit of it. He was staying only long enough to earn the money to settle some debts, and then he was going to leave for good. He was a good, gentle, hilarious man, and to this day I can't help thinking that he wasn't *supposed* to get killed in Vietnam, getting killed in a war was not John's scene, he'd made no room for that the way some others had. A lot of people I had liked a lot, GI's and even some correspondents, had already died, but when Cantwell got murdered it did more than sadden and shock me. Because he was a friend, his death changed all the odds.

In that one brief period of less than two weeks it became a war of our convenience, a horrible convenience, but ours. We would jump into jeeps and minimokes at nine or ten and drive a few kilometers to where the fighting was, run around in it for a few hours and come back early. We'd sit on the

"Well, I can't really stop you. You *know* I can't stop you. But if I could, I would. You wouldn't be driving up to no shit like those four guys."

In the early evenings we'd do exactly what correspondents did in those terrible stories that would circulate in 1964 and 1965, we'd stand on the roof of the Caravelle Hotel having drinks and watch the airstrikes across the river, so close that a good telephoto lens would pick up the markings on the planes. There were dozens of us up there, like aristocrats viewing Borodino from the heights, at least as detached about it as that even though many of us had been caught under those things from time to time. There'd be a lot of women up there, a few of them correspondents (like Cathy Leroy, the French photographer, and Jurati Kazikas, a correspondent of great, fashion-model beauty), most of them the wives and girls of reporters. Some people had tried hard to believe that Saigon was just another city they'd come to live in; they'd formed civilized social routines, tested restaurants, made and kept appointments, given parties, had love affairs. Many had even brought their wives with them, and more often than not it worked out badly. Very few of the women really liked Saigon, and the rest became like most Western women in Asia: bored, distracted, frightened, unhappy and, if left there too long, fiercely frantic. And now, for the second time in three months, Saigon had become unsafe. Rockets were dropping a block from the best hotels, the White Mice (the Saigon police) were having brief, hysterical firefights with shadows, you could hear it going on as you dropped off to sleep; it was no longer simply a stinking, corrupt, exhausting foreign city.

At night, the rooms of the Continental would fill with correspondents drifting in and out for a drink

chopper in until morning, you'd already picked a place to sleep for the night. Loon was the ultimate Vietnam movie location, where all of the mad colonels and death-spaced grunts we'd ever known showed up all at once, saying all the terrible, heart-breaking things they always said, so nonchalant about the horror and fear that you knew you'd never really be one of them no matter how long you stayed. You honestly didn't know whether to laugh or cry. Few people ever cried more than once there, and if you'd used that up, you laughed; the young ones were so innocent and violent, so sweet and so brutal, beautiful killers.

One morning, about twenty-five correspondents were out by the Y Bridge working when a dying ARVN was driven by on the back of a half-ton pick-up. The truck stopped at some barbed wire, and we all gathered around to look at him. He was nineteen or twenty and he'd been shot three times in the chest. All of the photographers leaned in for pictures, there was a television camera above him, we looked at him and then at each other and then at the wounded Vietnamese again. He opened his eyes briefly a few times and looked back at us. The first time, he tried to smile (the Vietnamese did that when they were embarrassed by the nearness of foreigners), then it left him. I'm sure that he didn't even see us the last time he looked, but we all knew what it was that he'd seen just before that.

That was also the week that Page came back to Vietnam. *A Scrambler to the Front* by Tim Page, *Tim Page* by Charles Dickens. He came a few days before it started, and people who knew about his luck were making jokes blaming the whole thing on his return. There were more young, apolitically radical, wigged-out crazies running around Viet-

try where the madness raced up the hills and into the jungles, where everything essential to learning Asia, war, drugs, the whole adventure, was close at hand.

The first time he got hit it was shrapnel in the legs and stomach. That was at Chu Lai, in '65. The next time was during the Buddhist riots of the 1966 Struggle Movement in Danang: head, back, arms, more shrapnel. (*A Paris-Match* photograph showed Flynn and a French photographer carrying him on a door, his face half covered by bandages, *"Tim Page, blessé à la tête."*) His friends began trying to talk him into leaving Vietnam, saying, "Hey, Page, there's an airstrike looking for you." And there was; it caught him drifting around off course in a Swift boat in the South China Sea, blowing it out of the water under the mistaken impression that it was a Viet Cong vessel. All but three of the crew were killed, Page took over 200 individual wounds, and he floated in the water for hours before he was finally rescued.

They were getting worse each time, and Page gave in to it. He left Vietnam, allegedly for good, and joined Flynn in Paris for a while. He went to the States from there, took some pictures for Time-Life, got busted with the Doors in New Haven, traveled across the country on his own (he still had some money left), doing a picture story which he planned to call "Winter in America." Shortly after the Tet Offensive, Flynn returned to Vietnam, and once Page heard that, it was only a matter of time. When he got back in May, his entrance requirements weren't in order, and the Vietnamese kept him at Tan Son Nhut for a couple of days, where his friends visited him and brought him things. The first time I met him he was giggling and doing an insane imitation of two Vietnamese immigration

ish and silly, he could be an outrageous snob (he was a great believer in the New Aristocracy), he could talk about people and things in ways that were nearly monstrous, stopping short of that and turning funny and often deeply tender. He carried all kinds of clippings around with him, pictures of himself, newspaper stories about the times he'd been wounded, a copy of a short story that Tom Mayer had written about him in which he got killed on an operation with the Korean Marines. He was especially vain about that story, very proud and completely spooked by it. That first week back, he'd had things brought around to where he could remember them again, remembering that you could get killed here, the way he almost had those other times, the way he had in the story.

"*Look* at you," he'd say, coming into the room at night. "Every one of you is *stoned*. Look at you, what are you doing there if it isn't rolling a joint? Grinning, Flynn, grinning is sinning. Dope is hope. Help! Give us a bit of that, will you? I ain't doin' no evil, give us just a toke. Ahhhhh, yesh! It *can't* be my turn to change the record because I've only just come in. Are any birds coming by? Where are Mimsy and Poopsy? [His names for two Australian girls who dropped over some evenings.] Women is good, women is necessary, women is definitely good for business. Yesh."

"Don't smoke that, Page. Your brain is already about the consistency of a soggy quiche lorraine."

"Nonsense, utter nonsense. Why don't you roll a five-handed joint while I prepare a steamboat for this ugly, filthy roach?" He'd jab his misshapen left index finger at you to underline key words, taking the conversation wherever his old child's whimsey took his thoughts, planning projects which ranged from full-scale guerrilla ops in New York City to

he and I spent ten days in the Delta with the Special Forces, and then we went to Danang to meet Flynn. (Page called Danang "Dangers," with a hard g. In a war where people quite seriously referred to Hong Kong as "Hongers" and spoke of running over to Pnompers to interview Sukie, a British correspondent named Don Wise made up a Vietnam itinerary: Canters, Saigers, Nharters, Quinners, Pleikers, Quangers, Dangers and Hyoo-beside-the-Sea.)

Page's helmet decor now consisted of the words HELP, I'M A ROCK! (taken from another Zappa song) and a small Mao button, but he didn't have much chance to wear it. Things were still quiet everywhere, fini la guerre, I wanted to leave in September and it was already August. We went out on operations, but all of them were without contact. That was fine with me, I didn't want contact (what the hell for?), that month in Hong Kong had been good in a lot of ways, one of them being the leisure it offered me to recall with some precision just how awful Vietnam could be. Away from it, it was a very different place. We spent most of August on China Beach sailing and goofing, talking to Marines who'd come down for in-country R&R, coming back in the late afternoons to the press center by the Danang River. It was perfectly peaceful, better than any vacation could be, but I knew that I was going home, I was short, and a kind of retrospective fear followed me everywhere.

In the bar of the press center, Marines and members of the Naval Support Activity, all information specialists, would gather after a long day in the IO Shop to juice a little until it got dark enough for the movie to start outside. They were mostly officers (no one under E-6 was allowed in the bar, including a lot of combat grunts whom many of us had

Vietnam after an earlier failure in the war. We rode around on those for a day and then took a boat downriver to Hue, where we met Perry Dean Young, a reporter for UPI who came from North Carolina. (Flynn called him "the fullest flowering of southern degeneracy," but the closest to degeneracy any of us ever came was in our jokes about it, about what bad, dope-smoking cats we all were. We were probably less stoned than the drinkers in our presence, and our livers were holding up.) Perry had a brother named Dave who ran the small Naval detachment that had been set up during the battle, directly across from the south wall of the Citadel. For months now, Flynn and I had been living vicariously off of each other's war stories, his Ia Drang stories and my Hue stories, and Perry's brother got a Navy truck and drove us around the city while I gave a running commentary which would have been authoritative if only I'd been able to recognize any of it now. We were sitting on the back of the truck on folding chairs, bouncing around in the heat and dust. Along the park that fronted the river we passed dozens of lovely young girls riding their bicycles, and Page leaned over and leered at them, saying, "Good mornin', little schoolgirl, I'm a li'l schoolboy too."

When I'd been here before, you couldn't let yourself be seen on the riverbank without machine guns opening up on you from the opposite bank, you couldn't breathe anywhere in Hue without rushing somebody's death into your blood-stream, the main bridge across the river had been dropped in the middle, the days had been cold and wet, the city had been composed seemingly of destruction and debris. Now it was clear and very warm, you could stop by the Cercle Sportif for a drink, the bridge

so acutely (some of us) that we understood what amputees went through when they sensed movement in the fingers or toes of limbs lost months before. A few extreme cases felt that the experience there had been a glorious one, while most of us felt that it had been merely wonderful. I think that Vietnam was what we had instead of happy childhoods.

During my first month back I woke up one night and knew that my living room was full of dead Marines. It actually happened three or four times, after a dream I was having those nights (the kind of dream one never had in Vietnam), and that first time it wasn't just some holding dread left by the dream, I knew they were there, so that after I turned on the light by my bed and smoked a cigarette I lay there for a moment thinking that I'd have to go out soon and cover them. I don't want to make anything out of this and I certainly don't want sympathy; going to that place was my idea to begin with, I could have left anytime, and as those things go I paid little enough, almost nothing. Some guys come back and see their nightmares break in the streets in daylight, some become inhabited and stay that way, all kinds of things can trail after you, and besides, after a while my thing went away almost completely, the dream, too. I know a guy who had been a combat medic in the Central Highlands, and two years later he was still sleeping with all the lights on. We were walking across 57th Street one afternoon and passed a blind man carrying a sign that read, MY DAYS ARE DARKER THAN YOUR NIGHTS. "Don't bet on it, man," the ex-medic said.

Of course coming back was a down. After something like that, what could you find to thrill you, what compared, what did you do for a finish? Everything seemed a little dull, heaviness threat-

on R&R in Vientiane when they were notified, and they flew immediately to Saigon. For nearly two weeks, friends at Time-Life kept me informed by telephone from their daily cables; Page was transferred to a hospital in Japan and they said that he would probably live. He was moved to Walter Reed Army Hospital (a civilian and a British subject, it took some doing), and they said that he would live but that he'd always be paralyzed on his left side. I called him there, and he sounded all right, telling me that his roommate was this very religious colonel who kept apologizing to Page because he was only in for a check-up, he hadn't been wounded or anything fantastic like that. Page was afraid that he was freaking the colonel out a little bit. Then they moved him to the Institute for Physical Rehabilitation in New York, and while none of them could really explain it medically, it seemed that he was regaining the use of his left arm and leg. The first time I went to see him I walked right past his bed without recognizing him out of the four patients in the room, even though he'd been the first one I'd seen, even though the other three were men in their forties and fifties. He lay there grinning his deranged, uneven grin, his eyes were wet, and he raised his right hand for a second to jab at me with his finger. His head was shaved and sort of lidded now across the forehead where they'd opened it up ("What did they find in there, Page?" I asked him. "Did they find that quiche lorraine?") and caved in on the right side where they'd removed some bone. He was emaciated and he looked really old, but he was still grinning very proudly as I approached the bed, as if to say, "Well, didn't Page step into it this time?" as though two inches of shrapnel in your brain was the wiggiest goof of them all, that wonderful moment of the Tim Page Story where our boy

at that, will you? Page is a fucking hemi-plegic," raising his cane and stumbling back to his chair, collapsing in laughter again.

He fixed up an altar with all of his Buddhas, arranging prayer candles in a belt of empty .50-caliber cartridges. He put in a stereo, played endlessly at organizing his slides into trays, spoke of setting out Claymores at night to keep "undesirables" away, built model airplanes ("Very good therapy, that"), hung toy choppers from the ceiling, put up posters of Frank Zappa and Cream and some Day-Glo posters which Linda had made of monks and tanks and solid soul brothers smoking joints in the fields of Vietnam. He began talking more and more about the war, often coming close to tears when he remembered how happy he and all of us had been there.

One day a letter came from a British publisher, asking him to do a book whose working title would be "Through with War" and whose purpose would be to once and for all "take the glamour out of war." Page couldn't get over it.

"Take the glamour out of war! I mean, how the bloody hell can you do *that?* Go and take the glamour out of a Huey, go take the glamour out of a Sheridan. . . . Can *you* take the glamour out of a Cobra or getting stoned at China Beach? It's like taking the glamour out of an M-79, taking the glamour out of Flynn." He pointed to a picture he'd taken, Flynn laughing maniacally ("We're winning," he'd said), triumphantly. "Nothing the matter with *that* boy, is there? Would you let your daughter marry that man? Ohhhh, war is *good* for you, you can't take the glamour out of that. It's like trying to take the glamour out of sex, trying to take the glamour out of the Rolling Stones." He was really speechless, working his

Breathing Out

I am going home. I have seen a lot of Vietnam in 18 months. May Lord help this place. DEROS 10 Sept 68.

Mendoza was here. 12 Sept 68. Texas.

Color me gone. (Mendoza is my buddy.)

Release graffiti on the walls at Tan Son Nhut airport, where Flynn, almost overtly serious for a second, gave me a kind of blessing ("Don't piss it all away at cocktail parties") and Page gave me a small ball of opium to eat on the flight back; stoned dreaming through Wake, Honolulu, San Francisco, New York and the hallucination of home. Opium space, a big round O, and time outside of time, a trip that happened in seconds and over years; Asian time, American space, not clear whether Vietnam was east or west of center, behind me or somehow still ahead. "Far's I'm concerned, this one's over the day I get home," a grunt had told us a few weeks before, August 1968, we'd been sitting around after an operation talking about the end of the war. "Don't hold your breath," Dana said.

Home: twenty-eight years old, feeling like Rip Van Winkle, with a heart like one of those little paper pills they make in China, you drop them into water and they open out to form a tiger or a flower

He spun on his heel and did it backwards for a few yards. Then he stopped and reached over his head. When he pulled his arm down a heavy rain came pouring in. "I been here so long I can call these motherfuckers in on the *dime.*" He put a lot of energy and care into his jive, it had made him a star in his unit, but he wasn't just some feets-do-yo-stuff spade. So when he told me that he saw ghosts whenever they went on night patrol I didn't laugh, and when he said that he'd started seeing his own out there I think I freaked a little. "Naw, that's cool, that's cool, motherfucker was be*hind* me," he said. "It's when he goes and moves up in front that you're livin' in a world of hurt." I tried to say that what he probably had seen was the phosphorescence that gathered around rotting tree trunks and sent pulsing light over the ground from one damp spot to another. "Crazy," he said, and, "Later."

They were bulldozing a junction into Route 22 near Tay Ninh and the old Iron Triangle when the plows ran into some kind of VC cemetery. The bones started flying up out of the ground and forming piles beside the furrows, like one of those films from the concentration camps running backward. Instamatic City, guys racing like crazy with their cameras, taking snaps, grabbing bones for souvenirs. Maybe I should have taken one too; three hours later back in Saigon I wasn't that sure whether I'd really seen it or not. While we were there and the war seemed separate from what we thought of as real life and normal circumstances, an aberration, we all took a bad flash sooner or later and usually more than once, like old acid backing up, residual psychotic reaction. Certain rock and roll would come in mixed with rapid fire and men screaming. Sitting over a steak in Saigon once I made nasty meat connections, rot and burning from

Marine, leaning in and staring with raw raving fear toward the incoming rounds; all four of us caught there together while Dana crouched down behind the camera, laughing. "You fuck," I said to him when he gave me the print, and he said, "I thought you ought to know what you look like."

I don't have any pictures of Dana, but there's not much chance I'll forget what he looked like, that front-line face, he never got anything on film that he didn't get on himself, after three years he'd turned into the thing he came to photograph. I have pictures of Flynn but none by him, he was in so deep he hardly bothered to take them after a while. Definitely off of media, Flynn; a war behind him already where he'd confronted and cleaned the wasting movie-star karma that had burned down his father. In so far as Sean had been acting out, he was a great actor. He said that the movies just swallowed you up, so he did it on the ground, and the ground swallowed him up (no one I ever knew could have dug it like you, Sean), he and Dana had gone off somewhere together since April 1970, biking into Cambodia, "presumed captured," rumors and long silence, MIA to say the least.

There it is, the grunts said, like this: sitting by a road with some infantry when a deuce-and-a-half rattled past with four dead in the back. The tailgate was half lowered as a platform to hold their legs and the boots that seemed to weigh a hundred pounds apiece now. Everyone was completely quiet as the truck hit a bad bump and the legs jerked up high and landed hard on the gate. "How about that shit," someone said, and "Just like the motherfucker," and "There it is." Pure essence of Vietnam, not even stepped on once, you could spin it out into visions of laughing lucent skulls or call it just another body in a bag, say that it cut you in half

Indian country. I slept like a morphine sleeper that night, not knowing which was awake or asleep, clocking the black triangle of the raised tent flap as it turned dark blue, fog white, sun yellow, and it felt okay to get up. Just before I flew back to Danang they named it LZ Loon, and Flynn said, "That's what they ought to call the whole country," a more particular name than Vietnam to describe the death space and the life you found inside it. When we rebuilt Loon on China Beach that day we laughed so hard we couldn't sit up.

I loved the door, loved it when the ship would turn a little and tilt me toward the earth, flying at a hundred feet. A lot of people thought it opened you to some kind of extra danger, like ground fire spilling in on you instead of just severing the hydraulic system or cutting off the Jesus nut that held the rotor on. A friend of mine said he couldn't do it, it put him close to rapture of the deep, he was afraid he'd flip the latch on his seat belt and just float out there. But I was afraid anyway, more afraid closed in, better to see, I didn't go through all of that not to see.

At midnight over Vinh Long, the gunship made seven or eight low runs above a company of Viet Cong on the eastern edge of the city. At first the tracers just snapped away into the dark, spending themselves out in sparks or skipping once or twice on the ground. Then flares showed a lot of men running out in the open, and our tracer lights began disappearing abruptly. The smoke from white phosphorus was so bright against the darkness that you had to squint a little to look at it. By four, half the city was on fire. Reporters weren't allowed on gunships, but this was the second night of the

came over and said, "Too bad we didn't get shot at. I'd like to've shown you my evade."

In the Special Forces A Camp at Me Phuc Tay there was a sign that read, "If you kill for money you're a mercenary. If you kill for pleasure you're a sadist. If you kill for both you're a Green Beret." Great sounds at Me Phuc Tay, the commander dug the Stones. At An Hoa we heard "Hungry for those good things baby, Hungry through and through," on the radio while we tried to talk to an actual hero, a Marine who'd just pulled his whole squad back in from deep serious, but he was sobbing so hard he couldn't get anything out. "Galveston oh Galveston I'm so afraid of dying," at LZ Stud, two kids from Graves having a quarrel. "He's all haired off 'cause they won't let him sew Cav patches on the bags," one said, and the other, pouting heavily, said, "Fuck you. I mean it man, fuck you. I think it looks real sharp." Only one song from Hue, "We gotta get out of this place if it's the last thing we ever do"; a reporter friend looking totally mind-blown, he woke up that morning and heard two Marines lying near him making love. "Black is black I want my baby back," at China Beach with IGOR FROM THE NORTH, every card in his deck an ace of spades. He wore a sombrero and a serape and his face went through about as many changes as a rock when a cloud passes over it. He almost lived on the beach, every time he added to the count they'd send him down as reward. He spoke twice in an hour in a spooky clipped language of his own like slow rounds, finally he got up and said, "Got to go Dong Ha kill more," and went. "I said shotgun, shoot 'em 'fore they run now," at Nha Trang, talking to a man just starting his second tour. "When I come home I seen how scared you all was. I mean it wasn't no damn combat situation or noth-

was growing older, I was leaking time, like I'd taken a frag from one of those anti-personnel weapons we had that were so small they could kill a man and never show up on X-rays. Hemingway once described the glimpse he'd had of his soul after being wounded, it looked like a fine white handkerchief drawing out of his body, floating away and then returning. What floated out of me was more like a huge gray 'chute, I hung there for a long time waiting for it to open. Or not. My life and my death got mixed up with their lives and deaths, doing the Survivor Shuffle between the two, testing the pull of each and not wanting either very much. I was once in such a bad head about it that I thought the dead had only been spared a great deal of pain.

Debriefed by dreams, friends coming in from the other side to see that I was still alive. Sometimes they looked 500 years old and sometimes they looked exactly as I'd known them, but standing in a strange light; the light told the story, and it didn't end like any war story I'd ever imagined. If you can't find your courage in a war, you have to keep looking for it anyway, and not in another war either; in where it's old and jammed until the rocks start moving around, a little light and air, long time no see. Another frequency, another information, and death no deterrent to receiving it. The war ended, and then it really ended, the cities "fell," I watched the choppers I'd loved dropping into the South China Sea as their Vietnamese pilots jumped clear, and one last chopper revved it up, lifted off and flew out of my chest.

I saw a picture of a North Vietnamese soldier sitting in the same spot on the Danang River where the press center had been, where we'd sat smoking and joking and going, "Too much!" and "Far out!" and "Oh my God it gets so freaky out there!" He